Thomas Nield

The Human Brotherhood and a Psalm of Faith

Thomas Nield

The Human Brotherhood and a Psalm of Faith

ISBN/EAN: 9783743351301

Manufactured in Europe, USA, Canada, Australia, Japa

Cover: Foto ©ninafisch / pixelio.de

Manufactured and distributed by brebook publishing software (www.brebook.com)

Thomas Nield

The Human Brotherhood and a Psalm of Faith

THE
✴Human✴Brotherhood✴

―AND―

A PSALM OF FAITH.

TWO POEMS.

By Thomas Nield.

THE CHURCH AT WORK PUB. CO.,
3½ East Washington Street, (Blackford Block,)
INDIANAPOLIS, IND.

COPYRIGHT, 1888, BY
THOMAS NIELD,
ALL RIGHTS RESERVED.

PROEM.

Whoe'er thou art whose eye may scan our page,
Prepare thyself to wrestle with the truth;
And if she throw thee, own the mastery
And thenceforth love her ardently, and serve.

Be thou a self-appointed censor, if
Thou wilt. Apply thy square and compass to
Our work; yet know its aim and purpose, and
Its architectural order, at the start.

We stand upon a promontory and
Behold the billows of a world, and fain
Would rear a lighthouse, that the nations may
Avoid the reefs where countless corpses lie.

We copy not the pyramids, nor Greek
Nor Gothic forms, but, building for the years
To be, with the materials at our hand,
Create an order of utility.

Our purpose on the front is clearly seen,
As night's queen-star upon her azure throne,
With enigmatic prophecies in rear;
The whole an ideal for the coming time.

Whate'er it be it is our own. For e'en
One's selfishness asks honesty ; since to
Attempt a literary theft, with a
Detective shadowing every line, were vain.

Then take it as it is for what it is.
If 'tis adapted to its purpose, well;
For 'tis perfection in the workman's style
To make his product serve the purpose sought.

In parting, listen to our closing psalm,
As to the echo of our former strokes
Upon the granite. May they leave within
Thy soul the impulse to a kindred faith.

CHAPTER I.

Scene—*On the Street.*

Norton.   Good day, Gillespie! for the day is good
That brings such tidings as this day has brought,
Though, like a welcome rain, it comes with clouds
   Gillespie.   'Tis good to meet you in so good a
      mood.
And pray what stirs your blood at such a rate?
   N.   An uncle on the other side the brine
Has bowed his head in answer to the beck
That all must heed, and left a competence
To me, his only heir.   Is that not good?
   G.   Congratulations multiplied.   Yet Time
Had more accommodated us had he
But swept his scythe a stroke ahead or back.
   N.   Yet blame no blessing after it arrives.
A tardy spring is greener when it comes.
   G.   It is a circumstantial paradox;
A lucky thing at an unlucky time—
Lucky for you, unlucky for the cause;
For I infer that you will have to leave.
Will you have time to help us organize?
   N.   The cause is not named Norton.   It will live

When we are with Methuselah.   But come,
Let's talk things over at the Balfour House.
                              (*They enter.*)
I hope to leave within a week; but you
Remain; and so there is a steersman at
The helm. This stroke of fortune gives us oil
With which to lubricate our new machine
And put us in good humor with ourselves.
    G.   That at your pleasure.
    N.   So I please. Meanwhile,
The program may be this: You organize,
As proxy for myself—the head and soul
Of all—and you will find the body move
Smoothly responsive to your grip of will.
First, trumpet forth our principles with such
A blast that men will think there must be force
At back of so much noise; for most men judge
Of movements as they do of bells—by sound.
The silent motions of the worlds are less
Observed than empty wagons on the street.
Next organize; make wise provision for
Supplies, remembering that the rills make seas.
I might myself bear all the burden when
Returned; but that which costs men nothing is
Esteemed at what it costs.   Watch carefully
The offices.   Get men whose souls are rock,
Through which our principles have worn their canons;
Not flabby men, who flap like flags the way
The wind blows, but your true men—such as have
The most uncommon share of common sense,

Who, though their flesh were ground to sausage-meat,
Would still be firm in soul. There are such men ;
And such a cause as ours deserves to have
Them, as it needs. And next, be diligent
In cultivating harmony, which is
The base of unity, which is the pledge
Of ultimate success and permanence.

   G. I feel already that our loss is half
Retrieved in what you leave us of your mind
To guide us in your absence. I shall do
The best I can ; which is but saying I
Shall act the man.

   N.   That is an angel's stent,
Your ideal's highest peak. I hope it may
Be Himalayan in its hight. I have but this
To add : Our cause demands your warmest faith,
Which is the strongest tonic zeal can take.
That cause rests on the right as on the rock,
And every principle we advocate
Is in a tower of truth impregnable,
From which our flag shall fling out fluttering hope
To all mankind. While I am absent let
That flag not lower an inch in token of
Obsequiousness to wealth. My stay shall but
Inure to the advantage of the cause
We represent.

   G.   How long do you intend
To stay ?

   N. Until I settle up affairs,
As well as learn the visual incidence

Of some who are the country's eyes. This done,
I shall return; and then look out for weights
Upon the throttle-valves, and whirling governors.

(Scene.—*Boylston Hall, England.*)

Mr. Bronson.—It gives me satisfaction thus to serve
Your uncle, who has been my friend; for in
The settlement of his estate I shew
Posthumous gratitude. Moreover, I
Am gratified to find his nephew such
A man of mind and character, who looks
With philosophic eye upon the broad
Horizon of affairs, and by the state
Of his deportment proves the worthy heir
Of one so worthy as my friend deceased.
Command my services to any length
That friendship's arm can reach.

Norton. Your kindness is
Appreciated to the final dot
Of gratitude. Allow this levy then
Upon your kindness; to procure for me
An introduction to some men of note—
Not the great dragon-flies that flit across
The surface of society, but those who feel
The motions of progressive thought, who are
The priests that give its oracles in word
And deed.

B. Circuitously I can serve
You there. Acquainted with the member of

Our borough, I can find you free access
To him, through whom your utmost wish may be
Obtained.
    N. The very thing I want, and which
Will earn you double thanks.
    B.   No, not at all.
I only thank your uncle in the deed
And shew appreciation of yourself;
In doing which I pay myself a honor.
    N. I feel that I am doubly rich in thus
Inheriting your friendship with the rest.

SCENE—*In a Parliamentary Committee Room.*

HON. WALTER FAXTON. Mr. Farley? Yes, acquainted from
A boy. My autograph will readily
Unlock this door—and lips. His grain, as you
Will find, is close and tough—not deal but oak.
An age that has the boast of such a man
Need not complain of poverty. But should
You find him in a gruff and grouty mood,
Distracted by dyspeptic tortures, deem
It not a personal affront; for now
His body is the tyrant of his mind.
The Irish member, Mr. Marvel—I
Can introduce you to him in an hour
Or so. A bill comes up this afternoon
In which he takes an interest; and
He will be there as sure as he will breathe.
Marvel is a conglomeration of

Intensity, with one idea as
A pivot where his being all revolves.
One from America needs little help
To reach his ear and heart.
    N.   Suppose you that
To-morrow he will have more leisure?
    F.   Yes,
To-morrow afternoon.
    N.   Then I will see
The sage to-day; to-morrow, Mr. Marvel—
That is, if fitting your convenience.
    F. 'Twill fit as nicely as the "i" in did. (*Exit.*)

    Scene—*In Mr. Farley's Study.*

Farley.—So you belong to the United States,
That void, or chaos of this hapless age,
Where what is horridest of saurian things—
With names and attributes congenialer
To monsters than to human things—crawls prone,
In the abominablest moral slime,
Or flaps its leathery wings in labored flight.
All things are in their inchoatest state—
Are tentativer than a baby's first
Essay to suck its toe—are jumbled in
Unjointedness—a heap of cobble-stones—
Self-magnified; greed, glorified; what is
Hideousest in character, in deed the
Damnablest, apotheosized, that a
Drivelling mediocrity may be
A crownless king. Humanity—the cant
Of cant! Democracy—the stenchfullest
Of all conceits! the cataract upon

The century's eye! What is humanity
Dehumanized? or what democracy
Where Judas is the equal of his Lord?
What but stark treason to the race and age?
    NORTON.—No worse than here, where Judas—he
        who holds
The bag—*is* Lord.
    F. An attic flavor there—
The creditablest repartee of many
A day. Your country has the attribute
Of bigness; it is bulk. Its history is
The history of an o'erblown bubble, that
May burst with any breeze. Its bulk is but
Unwieldiness. Withal, it lacks the pledge
Of permanence, in incohesiveness.
The portents of its judgment day are in
The sky.
    N. It has the common base of an
Original humanity. The rest
Are accidents of circumstance. *Perhaps*
We have the sweepings of your monarchies.
But we may utilize the litter you
Have made by your malgovernment, and from
The quarry of experiment bring forth
A fitting finial for the golden age.
    F. A dream—a chimera—a dragon's tooth
To tear you while you sleep. This hodge-podge will
But be so many diverse elements,
In diabolicalest effervescence, till
It settles flat, insipid—not a tang,

A scent, superior to its neutral staleness.
    N. Whence came your noble blood, your royal stock,
But from a kindred source, in darker days?
May ours not yet become a broader-based
Nobility, a vaster royalty?
    F. Yes, could you take the individuals of
The stock and isolate them from the rest—
Give them the sense of power, of worth, with all
Advantages of circumstance—from age
To age keep educating them with best,
Perfectest ideals in their eye; then take
Some one and make him isolateder
Than they, in the exclusiveness of a
Superlative condition, and keep up
The process, taking one, and one, and one,
Until the whole were idealized—then, sir,
It might. But not this muddle can avail—
Not this cimmerian, fog-dense, ink-black
Illiteracy; this premiuming of greed;
This throwing wealth among the crowd for them
To trample under foot in scrambling for;
This leveling that levels to the dirt.
    F. The Conqueror placed the pets of caprice on
The lesser thrones, and by his fiat made
Them noblemen. What need have all of us
But some more autocratic word to make
Us noblemen? some bloodier touch to cleanse
Our plebian taint and give us royalty?
But with experience for our oracle

We are content. Your faded fag-ends of
Nobility are held together by
Exotic threads, spun by the royal word
From common stuff. And royalty itself
Has often found itself in sorry straits.
Still, in the scale of sociology,
You strike the dominant by accident,
And I would resonate your note. If mere
Environment has made nobility
Of some, and royalty, it can of more;
And if of more, of all. Then were it wise
To furnish this environment to all
And so far forth ennoble all. Nor need
We balk before the task. The ages are
Our working hours. Your legislation has
Been downward for the multitude. The day
Of despots made the people slaves, and you
Assume their normal status is in chains;
And hence your legislation is for slaves.
We aim to legislate for all as men—
To get our jack-screws under them, in faith
That every hour will give an upraise to
The whole. May we not hope for opposite
Results to those obtained by you?

  F.   Hope? Ha.
Ha, ha! Yes, all infinity for hope
To flutter in and flap itself to death—
Room enough to rear aerial castles
That would house a million words. Hope! The
  young

Will hope. It is their manna as they pass
Through wildernesses toward a land they do
Not live to see. Yes, hope is angels' food,
But unsubstantial stuff for flesh and blood.
They hope for the impossible; and when
At last they come dead up against the facts
They are the astoundedest of all mankind.
Experience plays ichneumon with our hopes.
  N. And yet his vision on a watch-tower may
Be trusted more than his at bottom of
A well; and he whose aim is at the stars
Will clear the boulder at his feet.
  F.   Be sure
Your country sees with sober eyes or she
May view things with inverted sight. Enough.
Enjoy your dream and make the most of it;
But keep a lock on your Pandora box.
  N. We will, since you have let the evils out.

  Scene—*A Parliamentary Committee Room.*

  Hon. Mr. Marvel. Your country is the wonder
     of the world,
And well deserves that every honest man
Should breathe a blessing on its name. Ireland
Is debtor to its heart and purse; and 'tis
Her children's cynosure. We envy you
Your liberty and wait in weariness
The day when we shall share the boon as you.
  Norton. And you may wait and weary still before
     it comes.

M. I fear, yet hope; fo come it must.
The mills of justice must grind out our rights;
For e'en poor Ireland cannot always bleed.
 N. Give us as many people to the mile
As you, with self same types of social and
Domestic life, their duplicates in modes
Of toil, of thought, and all that constitutes
The texture of the man,—how much, suppose
You, would our country have to boast?
Suppose your country transferred bodily
Across the brine and soldered on to ours;
Incorporate it as a separate State;
Make every other State its duplicate;
Then give you all the liberty you dared
To ask,—how much would that improve your lot?
 M. Such questions—well they put the matter in
A speculative light. We can but guess;
And guessing in a case like this is blind
As catching midges by the moon; you miss
A thousand for the one you catch. Now take
Things as they are. Confront the ghastly facts.
That grin like skeletons while strangling us;
Then say if liberty, with all that it
Implies, were not a boon, as 'tis our right.
 N. Pray, what were liberty to those who lack
Self-help, ambition, loyalty, and the
Broad-breasted charity that holds the heart
Of liberty, giving the boon itself
Enjoys? What were *our* liberty were most
The people alien from the government

In heart? haters of law, because it made
The laws; chronic disturbers of the peace;
The greater, more illiterate, half against
The rest, with thirsty daggers ready, at
A wink, to slake their thirst in civil feud;—
In short, two-thirds the country living in
The seventeenth century?
  M.   Your colors are
Too dark—by far too dark. I must reject
The picture as o'erdrawn.
  N.   Too bold, perhaps,
Because the truth is nude. Well, veil it o'er,
And still the contour of the argument
Is there. Our people, though diverse, have still
A unity; though free, are loyal to
The government; and though tenacious of
Their creeds, are tolerant. Make yours as ours,
By educating them for liberty,
And that by training to the proper use
Of what they have, or 'twere a razor in
An infant's hands.
  M. I think her now prepared—
At least, for larger liberty; that nought
Besides so well can mollify her sores.
Self-government will give us confidence.
Respect our manhood and you make us men.
But we have been belittled, hectored, kicked,
And spit upon, as decent people would
Not treat a dog. And need you wonder if
We slouch the tail, or snarl, or even bite

A little now and then? By so much is
The soul of manhood in us still. Let us
Do less, we should deserve to be despised.
But what of it—prepared or unprepared?
Because a neighbor has a larger fist,
Must we submit to have her box our ears
And judge for us our fitness to be free?
No, we demand of her the common rights
Of common law that nations recognize.
Our right, sir—our inalienable rights—
Is that on which we plant our foot; and we
Resent the motherishness of tyranny.

   N. You give the truth in profile. Be the wrongs
Of Ireland what you think, she does by far
Too little; be they less, too much. Even
Resentment has its dignity. Much more
Does justice scorn the currish modes of spite
And claim her rights with noble front. At worst,
You echo but the wide world's dreary wail.
No other people but have suffered wrongs.
But never curses and assassin stabs
Redressed a nation's wrongs and burst her bands.
For every Boyne there's been a Flodden Field;
For every Drogheda a Cullodin.
But still the thistle blooms on Scotia's brow,
While Erin's harp hangs hushed in dusky halls.
Instead of highland thrift and happy clans,
Her glens and mountain slopes are heathered o'er—
A man-made wilderness—that deer may roam
Amid the ruins of a thousand homes,

To fusnish gouty epicures with sport.
And yet the nation neither sprinkles blood
Upon the skirts of the injustice nor
Sits still to grind a curse between her teeth.
E'en Albion is not free from Norman thrall.
Yet while she winces 'neath the yoke that chafes
Her galls, she knows that force is no emollient.
Which, think you, has the surest remedy?
    M.   Each nation has its own specific wrongs.
    N.   Admit refractive circumstances that
Occasion varied incidence.   One sun
Of opportunity has shone on both;
And Erin's song might be as sweet in tone
As Scotia's bloom is fair.   Of this herself
Gives proof.   One climate, soil and government
Pertain to all.   Hence all are favored or
Oppressed.   What upas then affects the south
And west?   What cornucopia pours in thrift
Upon the north and east?   Answer thus much,
The shell of your enigma will be cracked.
It must be other than the climate, soil,
Or laws.   Teach them that freemen are the free
In soul; that ignorance is slavery;
That no bad laws can equal anarchy,
And that the heaviest tax is indolence.
Teach them that Justice hears as well as feels;
That Reason has a mightier arm than Force;
And that the curse they breathe returns to them.
And teach them too that broadest brotherhood
Gives greatest strength; and that the time consumed

Upon the rent-flea might be better spent
Upon the rabid whiskey-dog that runs at large,
And while it bites the people breeds the fleas.
(Excuse the homeliness that brings truth home.)
These lessons learned, the land will have new life.
 M. I fear your heart is not with the oppressed,
And think you echo not your country's voice.
 N. I fear your worst oppressions have a smack
Of suicide. Who wastes a pennyworth
Of opportunity may seek in vain
For pounds. I fear the zeal that aims to cramp
Your sphere. The world's ascetic age is past,
And nations cannot live in hermitage;
Hence they are widening out their reach,
In faith that greater interests must include
The less. You yearn to narrow yours, and so
Out-blunder England, who forgets how much
Your weal is hers. Her welfare is in you,
Your life in her. You have a hand upon
The helm of interests belting all the globe.
Promote the whole you best promote your own.
The time is come to lift up man as man.
There is a rank oppression, with a reach
Extensive as the race, whose roots are in
Our brutishness; and from this banyan all
Oppressions branch. Though many-trunked it be,
The sap in all is *force*. The fabric of
Society is but a dovetailed scheme
Of wrong, that gives cupidity a place
Of refuge while it preys upon mankind.

Our highest ideal has been equal rights,
Implying right of power to do what is
Not right; an equal chance to trample down
The weak and stamp on them when down.
Our modes of government provide facilities
Whereby the whipster overfed may use
His wealth to snatch the starveling's morsel from
His mouth. We need a new political
Economy, and one whose postulate
includes a true interpretation of
The motto that has thrilled the world; and here
It is: EQUALITY OF RIGHT IN RIGHT.
Your spawn of legislative heresy
Is in your House of Lords, that fungi of
The obsolete. The ultimate of power
Is in their hands who, as so many gods,
Dictate the destiny of millions; whom
You have the power to serve but not control.
This hydra monarchy—this feudal ghost,
Makes children of the multitude;
And those who curse it from afar grow pale
To see it sheeted in prerogative.
Oft as it hears the midnight stroke of doom,
When an indignant country glowers revenge,
It grants a crumb and then evanishes.
But out it comes again and stalks abroad.
You need to lay it in the feudal grave
And let the ivy years consume its dust.
'Tis vain to hope for those to right your wrongs
Who feel the pulse-beat only of the past,

Who deem your poverty your normal state
And hang like leeches on your arteries.
   M. A ghost it is, at which but few would fire
A gun; that fifty curse where one would strike.
Because the country worships this fetich,
Aught less than an iconoclastic zeal,
Born of some desperate hour, would fail to rid
Us of the incubus.
   N.   These desperate hours
Breed blind men's remedies. You need not smack
The earthquake-lips of revolution o'er
Its corpse to break its power; than which you need
No more. Cast out the evil spirit and
Retain the body for a better soul,
To represent the country's second thought.
But let it represent, not monarchize.
   M. Your plan.
   N. First fix the number in the house.
As these decease elect successors in
And from the lower house for life. This would
Be democratic and conservative,
Both just and safe.
   M.   Though plausible.
Your scheme projects our remedy too far.
We want a present help for present needs.
The starving cannot wait for next year's corn.
   N. The quickest help is in a quickened pulse
And courage, such as on the wavering field
Sets heroes' eyes ablaze and snatches from
The hand of Death the blooming amaranth.

Who waits for Fortune never sees her face.

    M. We are impatient, sir, to grasp her hand.
We chafe for justice while we vainly wait,
As chafes the long-stalled charger under curb.
Yes sir; we want our rights, and want them now;
And we intend to get them as we live—
And get them by the shortest cut.

    N.   Excuse
Me if I seem to sermonize. And yet
Allow me to suggest, that it were well
Should prudence give you eyes. Have patience born
Of faith. Aim only at the possible,
Remembering that you have your hand upon
The crank of destiny; nor fear to strain
Your muscle on the crank. Think not to catch
A remedy, like butterflies, upon
The wing. Nations, like pyramids, must grow
With toil. You have the granite in your blood.
Develop that and you will grow apace
Until the country will amaze herself.

    M. There is a scent of reason in your words;
And yet I fear the substance is not there.

    N. Smell round a little and you'll find it near.

CHAPTER II.

SCENE.—*A Public Hall.*

GILLESPIE. We meet to-night with grandest aims
  in view—
To organize *The Human Brotherhood;*
Our object, to define and vindicate
The rights of man as man, and then devise
And use the means that shall secure those rights.
We need not gush in founts of eloquence,
Nor weave a web of subtle argument
From threads of sophistry, to prove a lack
Of balance in the opportunities
To share what nature has prepared for all.
On every hand we have our millionaires,
Not one of whom has given the tithe of an
Equivalent for what he holds; while most
Hold not the tithe of an equivalent
For service given. One has, but has not earned;
The other earned, but does not have. In such
A case, that eats the bread of this. The cause
Of inequality is radical.

The pendulum of a political
Economy that swings with such a sweep
As this, is out of line with equity.
To find that line, and then to make our beat
Equisonant, is that at which we aim.
And we invite the aid of all true men
In this the grandest effort of the age.
An honored friend, whom I had hoped to have
As president, is now in Europe, in
The interest of the cause; which throws on me
The burden of responsibility
For what we do; and this I willingly
Accept. Before we organize I shall
Be glad to hear what others have to say;
For here at least there is equality.

    ED. PRATT. It seems a mystery that we have not had
A move like this before. But here it is,
In proof that Justice has the breath of life.
What has been said is true, and mildly put.
Had those who, singly, waste enough to feed
A hundred eaten only what they earned,
They long ago had starved to death. They eat
And earn not; hence they eat what others earn,
And so are paupers. More; they waste and earn
Not; hence they waste what others ought to eat,
And so are vermin to society.
Behold their pomp upon the city's fringe!
With what an ostentation they display
The fruits of plunder, gained by tricks that have

The benizon of common sentiment
And all the guaranties and guards of law!
Plunder I say; for plunderers they are,
Taking the product of their fellows' toil.
With honest sweat we dig the treasure of
The earth; when they creep up behind and filch
It from us with a sly audacity.
What odds the law that gives its amen to
The deed? Can wrong be right because it wears
A legal livery? Tear from the deed
This vizor of legality, and turn
Them out upon the open seas, then let
Them there do what they do on land, behind
This thin disguise, and any nation would
Be proud to make them dangle from the yard-arm.
They would be pirates then. What are they now?
But here they face the day and sun themselves
Like peacocks, that mankind may stand agape
Before the glitter of their plumes. The law!
What an untrusty whirlagig it is!
Have not the laws been made by those who with
Their mother's milk sucked in the dictum, that
The right is as the sanction of the law;
Who then turned round and sanctioned wrong? We
    make
The men who make the laws. But we ourselves
Have been the slaves of custom. We must break
Our fetters and elect true men—such as
Will grind to dust, and scatter to the winds,
The social heresy, that they who have

The genius to impose upon their kind,
And by commercial sleight-of-hand
Extract the juices from their toil, should have
The privilege and be protected in
The deed; the heresy that idle craft
Has higher claims than plodding industry,
And that accumulated wealth, which is
So far an autocratic power, has a
Prerogative, in right, to use its powers
Still to deplete the common stock, drawing
A compound interest from society
On what it gained by the chicanery
Of trade. Here is the hellish essence of
This heresy: That right to hold is as
The skill to get; to use, as power possessed,
Within the limitations of the law.
To limit is to say the rule has bounds;
And hence the law itself concedes that power
Has not the right to wrong. The difference then
Betwixt ourselves and law is this—*the bounds*
Of right. An Alexander has no right,
By virtue of the majesty of might,
To get what is not his; nor Greedyfist,
By might of intellectual artifice.
Nor aught is theirs against the earner's will
For which they give no true equivalent.
And not a millionaire amongst us gives,
Or ever gave, the country this. Of course,
Men tell us glibly of the mind to grasp
The opportunities; the lightning eye,

So quick to see the chance to strike; the skill
To play the devil-fish and hide themselves
In ink, and take advantage by the smart
Exploit to do their fellows detriment.
This only tells how great the tiger is.
They have no greater than a burglar's mind,
A counterfeiter's skill; those cousins on
The other side the line of law. Not one
Has paid the price of what he holds. Take him
To Africa and what would he possess?
Perchance the tawdries of a medicine-man.
Then whence the plethora of wealth he claims?
It is the product of the manifold
Facilities that myriad other minds
Supply; which are the nation's common stock.
But these accretions of the ages he
Appropriates to himself, as one might claim
An instrument on proving skill to bring
Out Yankee Doodle. I inquire not here
About his skill—the burglar's forte;—but does
He have the right to thrust his hand into
The country's till, abstract its wealth and hold
It as his own? I answer, No. He *owns*
No more than a certificate of so
Much toil. The rest is legal pelf. We hold
This continent in trust, with all its stores,
For our posterity. A billion mouths
Will soon be opened to be filled. But we
Are trying, with a blind insanity
Of greed, to gorge the whole; and hence we see

This scrambling with distended claws—this craze
Of prodigality, before whose touch
Primeval forests fall, the hills grow poor,
And prairies lose their fat, that ones and twos
May put their tags upon the whole. The land
Is surely drunk. These men of millions earn
The execrations of posterity;
And should their memory last, its curse will be
Their epitaph. Such are the evils, then,
That claim our thought and call for remedy,
With thousand thundertongues of urgency.
A remedy may not be readily
Applied; and yet maturer thought must find
A remedy. The pressure of events—
Those whips of Providence—will force us on
To righteousness. But here I close.

  Tom Stone.   Well, chaps,
I'm not a speechifier; but I think
We needn't hunt a hundred lifetimes for
A remedy in such a case as this.
The shirks have got a thousand sneaking ways
Of keeping fat by trickery; for work
And they are mortal enemies. It's strange
They weren't too lazy to be born. No doubt
It tired 'em so it takes a lifetime for
'Em to get rested up. The only part
Of 'em that takes to work is tongue and jaw.
And so we have 'em peddling lightning-rods
And churns, washing-machines and books,
And patent humbugs just enough to fill

A dictionary; all a-snuffing round
A fellow's pocket-book, imagining
They have a fortune by the ear; and so,
I say, they wag their everlasting tongues
To have us keep them up in laziness.
And then our merchants bleed us on our goods;
And we grow lean while they are fat as pork.
And next, the landlords take their weekly toll
And screw us till they make us grunt. And then
We have the big-bugs—the monopolists
And millionaires—the leeches sucking like
They had a thousand mouths. Now I'm the one
To slam the door on all the tribe of shirks,
And sit down on the other fellows with
A slosh. It's no use talking, laziness
Has struck us like the cholera. It's no
Skin-deep affair. It's stuck right in; and it
Is spreading. Nearly every one's afraid
Of getting dirty hands, though not afraid
Of doing dirty meanness. And it's come
To this: men's pay increases as they get
Away from work toward stylish laziness.
It's time that something should be done; so I
Propose we organize and try to do it.

    JOBLINSKY. *Alias, the Dark Lantern.*
One man has talked of law, and I have faith
In law; for all we see and feel has law.
From sky, and earth and all that is, I learn
The ways of law; and so the way the laws
Of men should work. I look and see the cloud

That sits and on the sick earth looks so sad;
And while I look it bursts and fills the air
With fire and noise. It wipes its eyes from tears
And leaves us with a smile; and then the air
Is sweet, and earth is no more sick. And next
I look on earth, and there is filth and stuff
We do not want. We feed it to the fire.
That makes it smoke; and when the smoke is gone
The bad is gone. And so the laws of sky
And earth have taught me this: The foul wrongs
    done
By men must be burned up with fire and make
All clear, and clean, and sweet. Now men, the earth
Is full of wrong. The rich ride down the poor
And do them foul. And yet the rich live on
The poor, like lice on cows, and make them lean;
And so the poor are sick. And this is stuff
That fire could flame and clear the air. And there
I see a place to put the law. No more
I have to say; but when you want to do,
Count me two men for that.

    JOHN SWAB: *Alias, the Detective, a Hunchback Dwarf.*
                                Our meeting takes
A biologic course, evolving from
The chairman's one primordial thought, which was
A germ that now has variated on
To revolution. Evolution thus
Has evoluted to an r beyond
Itself. Now let us ponder o'er the fact—

Which science proves to be a granite fact—
That while conformity to type is writ
Most legibly on nature's page, and signed
And sealed by Fate, there is a tendence towards
Reversion to primordial types. And should
The vital modifier of the molecules
Become inert, our order will receive
A protophlastic trend; which monishes
To diligence. Be vigilant. Have more
Eyes than a dragon-fly, that looks all ways
At once; more constancy than gravity,
Which never tires.

 A VOICE. Don't elocute.

 ANOTHER.   I see
No 'cute about it.

 ANOTHER.   Let him go on. The
Dwarf knows p ain't pudding.

 THE DETECTIVE.   We need to watch
The genesis of things for inklings of
Development and help the lower forms
To variate aright. Get down then to
The crude bathybius of society
And, by gradations, from the polyp up
To consummated and sublimest life.
Our nature would impel us to array
Ourselves against the rich, until we may
Develop to an equal state. We must
Develop or become extinct, by the
Unerring law that sets its foot upon
The weakest with exterminating weight.

Now, as a vacuum is abhorred elsewhere,
So we ourselves abhor to be extinct.
Then try for an evolving impetus.

 The Smiler. I swan! but the detective is a great
Orthography gabblist, who heaps
Up capital in millionated words
And threatens a monopoly. Well now,
A simple chap like me can say his say
In words that are the wheelbarrows of speech,
And not mouth everlasting nothingness.
And here we need no *unabridged* to say
A rascal is no saint. We need not hunt
For scientific flummery to tell
That if we don't do something nothing will
Be done. Go to the mule and learn of him.
When an idea gathers in his head
It goes in lightning to his tail; and when
That member zig-zags, look for thunderbolts.
Let our ideas get into our heals,
Then kick and make monopoly see stars.
That is my plan for evoluting things.

 Bob Snag.—Look where we may are fellows
   wasting what
They have not earned. Full half their time is spent
Devising means of squandering money on
Themselves. Their wives and daughters are at
   home,
Dissecting aches, and analyzing throbs
And twinges, as they loll in luxury,
With troops of servants pampering them to death,

And docters tugging at the threads of life,
Blistering their pocket-books and dosing them.
These are the men that talk in lofty style
About the rights of capital. But what
Is capital? A god that we must bow
Before, and give our life to gain its smile?
What! we who dig the gold that makes the god
Bow down to it! The rights of capital
Are as the rights of stolen goods, except
As it is toil transmuted into gold.
The rights of capital are but the right
Of use for those whose toil it represents.
But we have chinned it long enough; and now
'Tis time we organize and set the truth
On fire, and bear it as a torch throughout
The land, to light us to a better day.

    SCENE.—*The Detective's store and a back room.*
    DETECTIVE. Come back, gents, to my private
        room. Take seats.
    BOB SNAG. What's up? I see your arm is slung.
    D.   Well sir,
This morning I was making a profound
Experiment upon my mule, and found
The creature contumaciously self-willed.
You see, that Nature, in her first essays,
Is homogenious, and, by gradual steps,
Keeps differentiating towards a type
Of greater heterogeniousness, in which
The royal intellect of man may aid.
And being of a scientific turn

Of mind, abreast with foremost thinkers of
The day, I tried to trim the creature's ears,
To give him more the semblance of a horse,
Hoping the other members would conform
To type. But at the first incision with
The shears, he seized my arm and almost crunched
It in his mouth, compelling my desistance.
    B. S. Would he have turned to horse or donkey
        do you think?
    D.   'Tis problematical. He shewed
Indeed reversionary tendencies.
    B. S. Well, that's enough of that. We have a
        plan
On foot. I reckon you can help to set
It up?
    D. I have the will to make the rich
Revert to their primordial place; and with
The will the way. You see, in buying up
Old clothes, I learn the situation of
A person's premises, which knowledge tells
Us where to plant the foot and strike. Oft as
Necessity demands I can afford
The information you desire.
    B. S.   Well now,
There's going soon to be a general strike
Of Longshoremen; and while it lasts we mean
To have no scabs sneak in and take the place
Of strikers. Can you help us there?
    D.   No doubt.
But first the strike. I will consider then

About the survival of the fittest.

JOBLINSKY. . Right nŏw I want your help of head
   and tongue;
For you, I see, can give the help I need.

 B. S. That's no affair of mine and so I'll go.
Well now, Detective, I'll remember this.

 D. And I will keep it in my secret drawer.
[Exit B. S.

 J. I want to purge a spot with fire. What rich
Man has the most that I can touch, and I
Will lay a red hand on that spot and make
A man of him who thinks that he is more.

 D. There is Gorman's up the river. I will
Go and point it out to you to-morrow.
On the way I'll tell you all you want to
Know about the man and place. Then you will
Be prepared to act.

 J. Act! That word is full of fire.
My head and heart are full of it. Act—Act.
My blood is hot, my bones are hot to act.

   SCENE.—*The Detective's back room.*

 DETECTIVE. How does the dark lantern work by
   moonlight? Did
You find the place exactly as I said?

 JOBLINSKY, THE DARK LANTERN. Just so. It was
   a place of pride, and ease,
And sloth, and waste. And now my heart says this:
That there I did a great proud deed of good.
I smote the proud and rich, that ate the poor
Man's bread, and purged a bit of wrong. I told

Not one, but went at dark and found the place,
When the round moon was red. And by our stream,
That seems so like a slice of sea that wants
To find the place it left, I sat where three
Big trees spread out as if to say, We hide
And tell no tales. Soon the round moon was white,
And made the night look like the ghost of day.
But at my back a hill spread out its black
Cloak where I sat and kept me hid. I saw
The bits of boats, both up and down the stream,
With flakes of light on them, that winked like eyes—
Like a child's eyes that nods and wants to sleep.
The small waves talked in low soft words that touched
My ear and made my heart feel soft. Live things
Were in the trees and grass, and all so glad
They had to tell it in their way. And loud,
And long, and sweet, a small bird piped so good
A note I could have thought a bee might suck
Some sweet from it. These made my heart more soft,
Till I was full of sweet weak soul—like girls—
And could have sat there all the night and wished
For no more day. Then came a boat, whose shriek,
And snort, and tramp, were as the rich man's pomp,
Who snuffs at all the poor. It scorned the rest,
And tost its waves, as though it shook at them
The spray from its proud feet. That woke my thoughts,
And made the blood of wrath burn hot and hate
It as a sign of wrong. But on it went;
And soon the swart hill hid the moon's fair face,

And laid its broad hand on the rich man's house,
And said to me : Black be its doom and deep
Its grave to-night. That was the sign ; and, like
The sign, I stole forth with a step so soft
It had no sound ; and ere the moon could see
The deed was done, and I lay down far off
And saw the smoke curl up, and then the blaze ;
And soon the red flames purged the black wrongs
    white.
Then jumped my heart, as jumps your dog to see
Your face, and wished that I could purge the world
With fire—the poor sick world, that has the rich
Man's bad, black ways to make it sick. Oh that
I had a life for each of my ten toes;
That these were ten times told ; and for each life
The power of ten ; and for each power ten worlds
To purge with fire! Then I should be too great
To be a man. The thought makes big my heart.
  D. You would evolve into a god. And who
Knows what we shall be yet? It may be this
Protuberance on my back is nature's seal—
A mystic pledge, or inkling of a change
Of type towards ultimate perfection ; and
A change in which the head will occupy
An inter-physical position, as
The focal point of intellect, and so
Make man a symbol of the infinite,—
His higher powers, as radii, rounding out
The circle of his being, that shall e'er
Expand, until the minds of men are great

As worlds. Nay, who can prove that all the worlds
Have not been so evolved? or that they will not
Still evolve until all space is filled—
An infinite conglomerate of life?
The great thoughts in me seem to work that way.
    D. L. Great thoughts come not to me; but when
        the rich
Man eats the poor man's bread, and treats him as
A beast whose back was made to bear his load,
My hate is hot and I would do hot deeds.
    D. Great thoughts will come to me like sparrows
        to
The eaves and make me reason thus: Since I
Am come, by numberless gradations of
Evolvement, from an inert molecule
To be the thinker of these thoughts, why not
Milleniums of evolvement make men gods;
And still milleniums of milleniums fill
Infinity with one sole god, of which
The separate godlings will be nerves, and he
The one, the brain of all? That would supply
The missing link that evolution needs.
    D. L. I think not thoughts like those, but of the
        things
I see and touch; and they are great to me.
    D. That makes me think this nebulous orb upon
My spinal axis is no accident
Of superfluity. Indeed, what is
A superfluity? Does Nature know?
Say rather, mortals misinterpret her

Initial motions in development.
The azure fields have none too many stars,
Nor earthly plains a blooming gem to spare;
Nor has my head a hair beyond its needs.
But beauty all, and harmony are in
Progressive stages towards a goal where, in
Imperial splendor, full perfection reigns.
In brief, I think that Nature takes, in me,
A forward differentiating step,
Or, otherwise, I should not have such thoughts,
With arms elastic as infinity,
Outreaching towards the still unreachable.
Oft as the afflatus of such like thoughts
Like lightning strikes, I wonder whether all
The scientists have like development.

  D. L. I know them not. But earth I know is not
A clam for one great throat to gulp, nor two,
Nor ten; but 'tis a loaf, made large, to give
A slice to each. Now can you tell me more
What spots to purge with fire?

  D.   Yes, I must help
You to supplant the saurian wrongs of earth
With better types of life and evolute
The race. Think of the dragons, lizards, and
The things whose names need two long breaths before
The tongue can leave the final syllable.
So hideous are the wrongs oppressing us.
'Tis infamous, infernal, damnable,

The way that most of us are forced to drudge
And, after drudging, scrimp and feel a void
Where they are billious with their gluttony.
I know a score of places that are but
Grand monuments of greed—extortion—theft—
Blood—death, whose grandeur mocks the poverty
They cause. These must no more offend our eyes.
They scandalize the spirit of the age,
And, like the irony that slaps us in
The face with love's own adjectives, provoke
Retaliation in a brusquer way.
We must retaliate. We must rebuke
The wrong or merit all the injuries that
We get, which, while the remnant of a soul
Is left in us, we cannot brook. Go forth
Then with your red hand well equipped, to strike
Humiliation to their haughty hearts.

    D. L. Strike? Yes, while there's a match to
        strike and I
Have one hand left; and I will give them woe.
And may the winds by day wail woe! And may
The black night weave a web of woe! And may
The hot lips of the fire say woe! And may
The white heaps of their wealth be weeds of woe!
And may their hearts be gashed by swords of woe!
And when their bones move may they creak with
    woe!
And when they think may all their thoughts be woe!
And when they hope may hope all turn to woe!

Scene—*On Main Street.*

Detective. Look at that carriage and the crea-
　　　ture in
It. Two fat horses—driver—footman—all
To draw about that puny burlesque on
Humanity, that is reverting from
The typic woman to an ape! See what
A pucker pride has put upon her lip!
And how her haughtiness has starched her neck!
She keeps a business sharper's wits upon
The strain to deck that dried-up carcass with
It's trumperies. The other week he had
A corner on the country's bread and squeezed
A hundred thousand from the poor man's loaf.
Oh the deep hellishness of such men's deeds!
Six feet of rope around his neck might do
A righteous deed. But lacking that, I'll shew
You where he lives. Then let him have a taste
Of his deserts, in fiery protest 'gainst
His wickedness. The preachers talk about
A hell. If hell there be, then hell is just,
And fire a righteous executioner; so let
Us forestall hell with hints of hell.

　　Dark Lantrn.　　　　　　　　O Fire!
Right's right hand! purge this bad man's deeds.
　　Scorch him,　　　　　　.
And leave a burn like live coals in his heart.
　　D. We need be careful here. The world has ears.
　　D. L. Yes, ears, like beasts of prey; and hands
　　　and heads—not hearts.

D.   Another geologic age
May evolute the heart.   Here, let us take
This car ; it goes within a mile of where
You want to see.   I guess we'll foot the mile—
At least, enough of it to shew the place.

   Scene—*In the public hall.*
 The President.   Over a hundred joined to-night.
   Now there
Is opportunity for some remarks.
Seeing, however, how much time is gone,
Let those who speak have some clear point
To make and stick to that.
   Jack Helms.   I've got a point ;
And see if I don't make it stick in some
Infernal rascal's hide.   I needn't tell
You that we railroaders are on a strike.
It happens so I know a thing or two
About some members of our company.
There's Tomkins, one of 'em.   He went out west
As agent to the Indians, and his pay
For four years came to sixteen thousand; out
Of which he saved a hundred thousand.   So
Much were the redskins in the lurch. Well now, ·
Had you or I but taken from his desk
One dollar of that hundred thousand, he
Who took it would have been a thief.   Then what
Is he who took the whole but so much more
A thief, who ought to wear his stripes and do
The state a little honest work?   And that
Aint all.   He went to Minnesota, where

He played another scurvy trick.   But first
He greased some congressmen with part of what
He stole, and got a land-grant for a road.
That done, he made a mighty blow, and
Got the state to issue bonds to help him build,
Then sold his interest for a million clear
And left for here, where he invested in
Our road.   And so the scoundrel comes to be
Our lord and have us in his power.   And since
His pile don't grow as he would like it, he
Intends to squeeze another dime a day
From us.   We ought to keep such scoundrels in
A cage, feed 'em an ounce of bread a day
And take 'em round to let the people spit
On 'em.   Now aint I made a point?

    BIG BILL.   That's so.
    OTHERS.   Bully for Jack!   That sticks.
    J. H.   And there is Quirk.
He got his pile by skimming Michigan
Of pine.   Whoever got the pine, he got
The butt end of the pay.   From there he stepped
Into Nevada, bought a hill or two,
Went east with specimens of silver ore
And made a boom for shares.   That netted him
So much he hardly knew.   With that he came
And got a big slice in our road.   And that's
Another of the precious scoundrels who
Have fleeced the country of its wealth, to live
In style and waste enough to keep the like
Of us in bread.   He too, the cormorant!

Would cut us down a dime a day. It takes
Fine genius to be smart as that! Neither
Has ever done a day's work in a day;
But, like a horse-thief, they have watched their chance,
While others slept, and ran away with what
The country owned. And now they've got their grip
Upon our throat, I tell you what—there must
Be some thing shaky with the law where such
Things are. I guess that where there is so much
Of ingrain scoundrelism in them e'en
Each seperate worm that feeds at last upon
There carcass will be struck with greed and want
    to gorge the whole.
  A Voice.   A taste would poison them.
  J. H. It's time that those who do the work should get
The pay; and I am in for anything
That shews a way of doing it.
  Dick Sledge.   Our road
Is owned by one—a thief, whose father was
A thief.
  A voice. There's grit.
  D. S.   It's true as truth can be.
Did either of them ever do more work
Than you or I to pay the country for
So large a slice? No sir! How have they got
It then? By playing business-poker down
In Shark Street. They were sharp enough, and mean
Enough, to gouge the country through the tricks

They played on others, when the sole return
They made us was, with thumb-and-fingers to
Their nose, to wink their compliments. Next, by
Degrees, they bought and bought till now they have
An iron collar round the country's neck.
The son has millions in the country's bonds,
For which he has not worked as hard as us—
The country's money in the country's bonds—
That he may settle grandly down and have
The interest fall in millions on him like
The dew—so easily it comes while he
Is smoking his cigar. Some simpletons
Have gushed themselves stone blind; because, for-
    sooth,
The country feels his cash. But every cent
    of it belongs to her; and being hers,
The interest is not his. Some blow about
His liberality; because a good
Streak takes him now and then, to give what is
Of less account to him than were a dime
To other men. What would we think of one
Who stole our purse, and from the interest on
Our money treated us to candy once
A year? Would we go slobbering over him
With compliments and laugh ourselves into
Ecstatic fits? I'd like to know what right
He has to spend some thirty thousand in
A night's display, to glorify himself,
As though he were the god of wastefulness,
While leaguing with the rest to scrimp us in

Our pay, whose labor foots the bill and keeps
The country on its pins. He gets, per year,
The pay of twenty thousand men. Does he
Return as much as they for what he takes?
Or is there the equivalent of them
In his one hide? Nay, is there of a score?
No sir! I'd like to try him on the road
A day. Then his excess is either too
Much by so much, or what we get too little.
Such things are an infernal shame. I tell
You boys, I'd like to smash the rascal's snout.
I move that we resist them to the death;
And let them keep their precious bones indoors—
The vermin that they are!

    Bob Snag.   I only know
That those we work for get what others earn.
They get the corn and we the cob; and now
They want to nibble down the cob. But we
Ain't going to submit. We're just chock full
Of fight, and there'll be blood a-leaking if
They don't look out. A dog's a worthless cuss
That has his tail stepped on and won't shew fight.
They step on ours, and we have filed our teeth;
So let 'em watch their shins. And now, if we
Can help things on I hope we will.

    Dark Lantern.   Such men
Are warts that earth wants not. A spark of fire
Would take them off the skin; and I for one
Will help to take them off. Speak on and I will do.

    President. The time is come to close. We hope

The day will come when, in exigencies
Like this, we may afford substantial aid
To those who struggle with the tiger-powers
Of wealth. At present we can only give
Them sympathy and words of cheer—which have
Their worth—and these we give as sacredly
As holy water from the stoups of our
True hearts. Their cause is just; and even should
They fail in this attempt, they must at last
Obtain some fair adjustment 'twixt themselves
And those whose lordish tyranny now treads
Them down. Ages have burned their incense round
Oppression's altar; but his doom is sure.
Sure as the stars are in the silent blue,
A mighty change will come. Not always can
This country halt the way it does. We have
Too much of liberty to get no more;
Too much of power to be forever wronged.
Our fathers found a continent that teemed
With wealth—with mines and forests ample for
Our needs, and fruitful acres that can fill
A billion mouths. These cannot always be
A common plunder for rapacious wolves.
If not our judgment, our necessities
Will bid the greed of money-maniacs halt.
The old-world notions of the rights of power
Must yield before the claims of equity.
Since this is thought, it is begotten; since
'Tis just, it is a germ of life; and since
It lives, the years will bring it to the birth.

What has evolved from past conditions is
A guaranty of full equality.
Our mission is to aid in that evolvement.

The Detective. Congratulations, Mr. President, for
Using scientific terminology,
Which is the summit, yea, the highest peak
Of speech. We are evolving in the style
Of our discussion; and I hope that in
The subject matter we shall witness a
Survival of the fittest at the last.

The Smiler. I move that we evolve ourselves
away;
For I resolve that I'll evolve for home.

Scene.—*The Detective's back room.*

Detective. You gave my lord an evening call
and left
Your card illuminated well. No doubt,
He will remember it. How did you get
Along in paying compliments?

Dark Lantern. Most well.
The night when all the signs had tongues that said,
Go on, I went; and dark it was—so dark
It hid me in its cloak, and hid the stars.
I heard the dog you told me of. He barked
And shook his chain, which told me where he was.
I crossed the wall and threw at him some meat—
The kind that cures the barks—and then lay still
And heard him eat the meat. I lay and lay,
And heard him whine and scratch; then all was still.
By that time I was stiff with cold, and rose

And stretched my limbs. I had been sick with
    thoughts
That found my mind and asked no leave, but walked
Right in and shut the door. Their face was sad
As if a friend were sick, and made my heart
Go thump. What if a babe be in that house?
They said. Can that be good which burns it up?
Can that be pure which blots a pure life out?
No no! I said; so proud a jade as that
Can give no spark of life, with Death's hand on
Her own. She is a speck that sticks to earth,
Like dirt, and makes us want to cleanse the earth
To take it off. What if the minx did burn?
The world would but be rid of so much wrong.

    D. I vow, Joblinsky, but you almost had
A woman's squeamishness.

    D. L.   What, were I one?

    D. You would have had a wishy-washy heart
And shrunk away.

    D. L.   Ah well, you seem to know.
But as I thought of her and saw her mince,
And toss her head, and hook her nose, and screw
Her lip, and stab me with her eye, my heart
Grew strong. My cold blood warmed and got on fire.
That, said my heart, is what will cure the pride
And make wrong right. It was my sign. I found
A shed, and coal, and wood. The night was then
As if the sky had shut one eye and left
The light of one. I made a heap of things
That burn; and when I stood a long way off,

I saw the big blaze burst and flap its wings
In the deep dark. And soon came screams and shouts;
And then I hoped the speck of dirt was gone.
    D. Bravo! The times demand that wealth should be
Rebuked. We must destroy the whip of power
Rather than have it plied upon our back.
You overcame the woman in your heart
And let the man develop strength. 'Tis well
To watch reversionary tendencies.
Unless we did we all might turn to women.
    D. L. You seem to rate her low. What is she in your mind?
    D. Only a bit of nervous stuff,
Which palpitates and screams, and weeps and faints,
And dies a thousand times, then lives to spite us.
And more 'tis so the more you pamper her.
She makes a study of herself and thinks
Herself a fragile thing, which everyone
Must handle like a snowflake, lest she melt.
I sometimes look at her and wish that sex
Could differentiate to give her strength.
    D. L. The truth in what you say half makes one mad.
Yet all are not like that.
    D.   I never saw
One otherwise; which may be my misfortune.
At all events, it proves the rule.
    D. L.   One I

Have seen whose nerve is strong, whose heart is
    brave
As mine; and she would dare as much.
    D. It cannot be. What contradicts the laws
Of nature cannot be; and nature in
An age like this is taken at her worst—
At least, so far as woman is concerned;
And so I more than doubt, I disbelieve.
    D. L. But I can tell you that it *is ;* and that
Which is can be.
    D.   That would be womanhood
At its ideal hight. Could I meet such
She might develop love in me. But not
Your waxy touch-me-not, who would collapse
As touched with fire if you unloosed her corsets.
Give me a brave heart in a woman's breast
And you have found me nature's masterpiece.
    D. L. If aught I know, I know that I could find
    one such.
    D. You have not touched her heart or you
Had felt it flutter when she saw a mouse
Or felt a spider crawling on her neck.
    D. L. 'Tis true, I have not touched her heart;
    and yet
I would not boast my heart more brave than hers.
    D. To be acquainted with her I would give
The best I have.
    D. L.   Tut! would you give your heart
And so be poor?
    D.   If she accepted there

Would be exchange, and I should be enriched;
If not, I could not lose. But I must prove
Her mettle to believe.
    D. L.   I know her well.
There is on earth no friend I love so well
As she.
    D. Your sweetheart, eh?
    D. L.   Not as you mean;
Nor can she be; as I could tell you why.
    D. Ha ha! I see. Your sister.
    D. L.   No, not that;
And yet as dear.
    D.   Then I can love her on
Your word. Indeed, my heart already is
As when the sunshine strikes an icicle—
Inclined to melt with warm impassionment.

    D. L. Now, by the bonds that bind us, be it as
You say. You yet shall see her eye to eye.
Then blame me if she be not what I say.

(*A boy sings at the door.*)

        Love's blind the people say;
        But hate is blinder still.
        This has so strong a wont,
        And that, so weak a will.
        And hence, in all they do—
        Since passion is so strong—
        The loved is always right,
        The hated, always wrong.

Though hate is super-blind,
Revenge is blinder still.
This has a madman's hand,
And that, a madman's will.
And hence, between the two,
Is passion doubly strong,
To frown upon the right,
And strike to do the wrong.

D. Love—hate—revenge. He runs the gamut of
The feelings. But his accompaniment is false.
Such songs are sentimental emptiness—
The clippings of a poet's dreams. That's all.
(Enter Bob Snag.)
B. S. We want your help to clear away a scab.
You lay the trap and we will take the rat.
To-morrow, Thursday, is a lucky day;
So do it in the dinner hour, and I
Will call on you and learn the ins-and-outs
Of what you've done. The one that has the spot
Is Ben Boyle, foreman of a gang on
East side, loading up the Great Mogul. We want
To teach him what it costs to keep us out
Of work, and give the rest a hint that they
Can take.
    D. Say what you want and here's your man,
Ready at all times for heroic deeds,
With sharpened shears to give a clip on call.
You never catch this weasel in a nap.

B. S. Then lay your plans, that we can catch
   him on
His way from work and clean him out as though
The earth had swallowed him. I know the boys
Will give you lots of custom for it.
   D.   Good.
The sly old rat may find his match this time.

SCENE—*By the east side docks.*

DETECTIVE. Now don't you want to treat your-
   self to day?
Here is a pair of pantaloons that must
Have cost five dollars, new. I bought them from
A big-bug's servant for a song. And see—
The newness of the nap is on them still.
Well, as I got a bargain I will give
One too. You can have them for two dollars.
Cheap as dirt and good as gold.
   BOYLE.   Not to-day.
   D. I want to sell you something anyway.
Come here. Come. Well, I want to tell you
   something.
(*Whispering.*) I've got the wind of something you
   have need
To hear. This way. (*B. follows.*) The strikers
   have a plot
Against your life.
   B.   How do you know?
   D.   Don't ask
Me how I know. I know, and that's enough.
I've told enough to make my life not worth

A cast-off shoe if they should find it out.
Their plan is this: when all of you quit work
To-night, they mean to make a feint of an
Attack on all the gang, but let the rest
Escape and do the job for you. Now don't
You squeal on me or I am gone.
    B.   Not while
My name is Boyle.
    D. I know their plans so well
That I can shew you to a certainty
The way to trick them all. See, come up here.
      (*He goes.*)
Now, when you quit to night, just make your chance
To sneak away up here alone, between
These piles of lumber. This, you see, is plank,
That siding. That in front of us you'll have
To climb. That brings you to the street; then use
Your wits and legs and you are safe. It makes
Me laugh to think how nicely you will block
Their game. (*Laughs.*) Won't they be riled for
       once! But note
The place as you regard your life and cross
Right here.
    B. I will. A thousand thanks to you.
Be sure I won't forget you after this.
But I must hurry back and shew myself.
          Scene—*In an old shop.*
    Bob Snag. I tell you, it's a tarnal shame to have
These scabs come in and take a fellow's bread.
Ain't these infernal imps of greediness

A-squeezing us to death? And when we make
A move to help ourselves these scabs are there
And help to make their villainy succeed.
I tell you boys, we have to fight or starve.
We have to whip them or be whipped ourselves.
It's come to be a thing of life or death
With us. And when it comes to that, are we
The stuff for them to walk right over and
To blow their nose on us? I ask you, Shall
We sit and suck our thumbs, with families
A-starving, inch by inch, when we can help
Ourselves?

 THE OTHERS. By thunder no. No sir. Not much.

 B. S. Then we shall have to give a claret hint;
And if they can't take that, another and
Another till they let us well alone.
They've started in, and let them blame themselves
For what they force us to. The fault is theirs,
Not ours.

 JOE BLACK, *alias* BLACK JOE.—Well, what do you
  propose?

 B. S.   There's Boyle,
That bosses this infernal thing. He is
The anchor of the whole concern. Get rid
Of him, the cable's cut and all the rest
Will drift. Now who will volunteer?

 SLIM SAM.   It is
A serious thing to take a human life,
Which, taken, cannot be restored.

 B. S.   I'm glad

You see it as a serious thing; for here's
A game where lives by hundreds are at stake,
And this mean scab would come and sweep the
    board.
Our lives are threatened; and myself and Bob
Have other lives at stake. I swan it *is*
A serious thing. And who's to blame but him?
His action is a challenge; and shall we
Be mum and die, as monkeys drown, without
A move? Not if I know you Sam.

  BIG BILL.   That's so.

  B. S. He stakes his life, and we are giving odds;
So I propose that we shall play the game.
I'm ready with an ace to cover him.
I've fixed the thing and only want some help.

  B. JOE. How many will you need?

  B. S.   We four can do
The job up neat and earn the thanks of all
The boys.

  B. JOE. Is everything in ship-shape? It's
A job that must be finished when begun.

  S. S. Yes, have you got it safe?

  B. S.   As safe as a
Mosquito 'tween one's thumb and finger. Let
Me see—it's nigh on half past four. Now boys,
This chance or we are whipped; and hell knows
    what
Will come of us. Who's ready for the job?

  B. JOE. Here's one.

  B. B.   And me.

S. S.   And me.

B. S.   That's business. Now
I'll shew you to the place and tell the plan.
Then we mast scatter and return by ones,
When I will shew you how to do the thing.
But first a treat for luck; so come along. (*Exeunt.*)

                 Scene—*In a lumber pile.*

Slim Sam. Thunder! but he's an everlasting while.

Bob Snag. He's sure to come; you watch your corners well.

S. S. I swear but this is scaly work. I guess I wasn't made for this.

B. S.   It's not our fault.
They force us to it; and it's only what
They're doing in a slower way. You see,
He's boss; he eggs them on; and if we fix
Him that will warn the rest and may-be save
A score of other lives as well as ours.
No telling what may happen if we don't.
Besides, it's me and Joe to fix him up.
You only—sh—here he comes. Now for
Showing who is boss. (*Boyle passes between the lumber piles. Big Bill and Slim Sam step before him.*)

Big Bill. Good evening Ben. (*In turning, he is struck by Bob Snag and falls.*)

Brack Joe. (*Striking.*)   One more
To make it sure. All hands. (*They throw him into the water.*)

B. S.   Good-by old cuss! (*Exeunt.*)

Scene.—*In the old shop.*

Slim Sam. That fellow's looks keep hounding me
both day
And night, and which is worse, the day or night,
I hardly know. 'Did you hear him when he
Struck the water how he groaned?

Black Joe. No, that was
No time to clear my ears of wax, and hold
My hand behind my ear, to filter groans.
My business called me to another place;
So, when he splashed, I thought of number one
And let him have the best my legs could give.
The job was neatly done. That's all I know.

S. S. I tell you, but I heard him groan—and such
A groan! Not one that has a lusty pain
At back of it. It was as though a soul
Groaned, and my soul responded with a groan,
That lifted up my scalp and made a chill
Go tingling through my skin, and pricking pains
At bottom of my back strike inward. Then
The sweat poured out and I let out from there.
That groan has left its ghost within my ear
And haunts it like a murmur in a shell.
Last night, it was the staple of my dreams.
I heard the wind blow; and it blew in groans.
I stood beside a cataract; and as
It struck the bowlders, every bowlder groaned.
I stepped sheer o'er a precipice, and woke
Like one who has the ague; and I saw
His face the way it looked when he perceived

That you and Bob were back of him. My soul!
I hope I may not see the like again.
I couldn't sleep another wink. I durstn't sleep;
And so I walked the floor. And even now
It makes my stomach sick to think of it.

 B. J. Oh fudge! Don't be white-livered now it's
  done.

 S. S. Well, fudge or no fudge, it has followed me
To-day so closely that I've turned upon
The street to see when there was no one near. (*Enter
Bob Snag.*) Gosh! how you made me start.

 B. J.   Sam's got a touch
Of chicken fever.

 B. S.   Chicken fever, eh?
Well, time has got a score of cures for that.
It's like a child's first bugaboo that makes
It shy for weeks. Before he lives to be
A hundred he will find that life means war;
And every fellow has to fight to hold
His own. When he gets pounded round the-world
Like me, I guess he wont spend days and nights
Trying to manufacture pity for a wretch
We struck in standing for our rights. He'll find
That pity needs to roost at home.

 S. S.   I don't
Know that; but if my hands were clean 'twould be
A long, long day before you caught me in
A scrape like this. Some men aint made to kill,
And I am one of them; and how on earth
I came to have a hand in it I don't

Begin to see. It's queer what spells one has
Of playing fool. I guess the difference twixt
Men is, that some are always fools; the rest
Are fools sometimes.
  B. S.   My gracious granny! What
A streak of blue you've got around your lip!
You must have had the colic in the night.
Why, Sam, you're not beyond the baby stage.
You need to have your gristle turn to bone
Before you face this rough-and-tumble world.
Blue! Why a fellow ought to laugh to think
How nice a job we did, without a track.
I'll trust the water for the tales it tells.
Golly! but wont they scratch their heads and feel
A trifle ticklish when they find no Boyle?
I guess they *have* enquired a score of times,
"Where's Boyle?" "Has anyone seen Boyle?" Ha!
  ha!
It must be better than a penny show
To see how colicy the crowd is now. (*Enter Big
  Bill.*)
  B. B. Have you heard it?
  B. J.   Heard what?
  B. B.   The peelers have
His body.
  B. S. By thunder! How do you know?
  B. B. The boys says so, they do.
  B. S.   That springs a leak;
For now they'll all be wide awake for tracks. (*A
  pause.*)

B. S.   Keep cool as cucumbers on ice and don't
Be seen together, then we all may wink
And whistle Rory-o-more.

B. J.   Sam, how pale
You look!

B. S.   What! got the inside shakes? Come now,
Be chirk and sing, When my old granny was
Young. Tighten up your jib and starboard helm.
Listen and hear the old brass rooster crow.
Why Sam, we didn't make the world, but found
It cut and dried, and have to make the best
We can of what we have. If now and then
We get a leathery piece to chew—why, get
The juice out if you can, or if you can't,
Just swallow it.   But anyway, don't puke.
Pshaw! you're like a tombstone—white, silent, and
Your face a solemn epitaph that tells
Of the departed soul. Now shake your dust
And come to life again.

S. S.   I reckon we
Must make the best we can of it, if best
There be.

B. S.   There now, there now! That sounds like
 Sam.
Another sweat will bring you out all right.
Come, take a glass; I'm not quite out of chink.
   (*Exeunt.*)

   SCENE.—*The Detective's back room.*

DETECTIVE.   Where is the lady friend you told me
 of?

I hoped ere this to feast my eyes and heart
Upon the highest evoluted form
In earthly guise.
 DARK LANTERN. Ah! now I see you joke;
And men daub not with jokes what has the best
Place in their heart, but wash their hands when they
Would touch its robes.
 D.   By all that's great, I do
Protest you misinterpret me. I love
Her on your word; for though the visual sense
Has not received her form, the attributes
That glorify the form are such as make
Her glorious in my eye—more glorious to
My heart. When can you give an introduction?
 D. L. I might to-day. But should her heart go out
To you and find that yours is ice she would
Be sad; and words would not have power to tell
How sad my heart would feel for her; for I
Have none on earth more dear.
 D.   Since you can love
Her so she must be worthy of my love;
For we are so alike that what can warm
Your heart can not be cold to mine Tell me
Her complexion.
 D. L.   As fair at least as mine.
 D. Her eyes—have they the deep black luster that
Bespeaks volcanic fires, or the mild blue
In which one looks for quiet stars aad soft
Etherial attributes like summer clouds?

  D. L. I need be proud if mine be grey and deep
With strength of soul as hers.
  D.   Ah! like the clouds
That nurse the lightning in electric arms.
And has her hair the flaxen glossiness
Of yours, so like the tint of amber clouds?
  D. L. I hope that mine is rich and fair as hers,
That you may think as well of it.
  D.   I think
Your hair is worthy of your character.
Rich hue, deep soul. I always did admire
Your hair.
  D. L. Then hers is sure to please you well.
  D. What is her contour? delicate in grace,
Or brawny, like her soul?
  D. L.   It suits me to
A dot.
  D. Then there must be affinity
Between the two; for only kindred souls
Can find their ideal in each other thus;
And that still glorifies her character.
For you I deem a most uncommon man;
To say which need not bring a blush to warm
The cheek of modesty. You are too strong
For that.—I vow, Joblinsky, you have fired
My heart as never was before. I must
Be introduced to her. But do you think
It probable she will reciprocate
My love?
  D. L. Ah now! You read my heart and I

Will tell you hers.

D. Of course. Yet, knowing both,
You have a base for an opinion.

D. L. You need
Not fear; for she can love a great high soul
That hates the rich and proud and smites the wrong.
But she has such a heart that she would want
All yours.

D. That's noble, brave, and just to ask.
It shews the greatness of her soul; for which
I but admire her all the more. She is
A queen to rate herself so royally—
A sage with so acute a sense of right.
To her I consecrate my heart to its
Last atom—yea, to its last particle
Divisible.

D. L. Then you shall see her face.
And now, what work of good have you to do?

D. Prudence has put her finger to her lip,
And Caution bids us halt a little while,
Until the opportunities evolve
From the volcanic chaos of affairs.
The longshore strikers have to lick the dust.
The railroaders may have to do the same.
And now the tyrants have their hirelings out
Snuffing for tracks in every secret place.
But how soon can you bring your lady friend?

D. L. What! will your deep love drown you
should I not?

Now this I bid you do: look in my eye

And see her as a soft cloud in a lake,
Which ia the ghost of what is in the sky.
Kiss me and she shall have that kiss from you;
And when you give to me my soul will give
You back as good a kiss.

    D.   What! kiss a man
And think I have the nectar of so grand
A woman's lips!

    D. L.   Let your soul give it and
My soul will make it sweet; for her you kiss
Through me.

    D. 'Twill be adulterated honey.

    D. L. Call me the comb and say you get it pure.

    D. Here then I kiss you, and the thought of her
Gives sweetness to it. (*Kissing Joblinsky.*)

                                    Oh sweetness! you kiss
As though her soul were in your lips. Do let
Me see her quickly as you can.

    D. L.   Her soul
Is here for all that we can see, as friends
Are with us in our dreams. Why not?

                                    (*Enter Jack Helms.*)

    J. H.   We're whipped—
Tarnationally whipped, from head to foot.
But then we shewed our grit, and that is worth
One licking anyway. Well, luck ain't all
Upon the boss's side the penny. They
Have had their toss-up, and we may have ours
And change the heads and tails. Wait till we get
A million strong, or more, and see if they

Don't have to touch their hats to us and say,
"Please gentlemen." I hope to see that day.
See here Joblinsky; have you got a match?

 D. L.   Yes, all you want, and one or two to spare.

 J. H.   We want it somewhere after dark, and the
Dark Lantern there to strike it.

 D. L.   Ah! I see.
No need to grease a stream to make it flow.

 J. H.   All right. We'll shew you where the channel is.

CHAPTER III.

Scene.—*On Shipboard.*

Mr. Bunco. Both of us returning to the States. You
Are from?

Mr. Norton. New York.

B. The Empire State; and I
From Hoosierdom—two of the brightest stars
That glitter o'er the stripes; no little boast
Where all are so magnificent. Is not
The States the marvel of the world?

N. I guess
The world is rather reticent upon
That point; at least, I have not heard the world
Express herself.

B. That's tally one for you.
But really, the like was never seen—
The way things go ahead. It's touch and go
In everything. Look at our matchless wealth—
Enough to make the world feel beggarly;
The grandeur of our commerce—interstate
And foreign—what can equal it? Our mines,
Forests, farms—everything upon a scale
That whips creation out of countenance.

No wonder brother Jonathan is tall,
With such a stimulus to pride. It is
Enough to make a hunchback straighten out;
Enough to warm a toad at Christmastide.
    N. What genius does it need to spend from a
Full pocketbook?
    B.   But then the life—the life
And energy there is in everything!
No plodding, dawdling pokiness that
Lets its shadow run away from it.
Up while the sun is putting on his clothes,
And pop and go all day, like lightning with
A thunderghost behind it. Wonderful!
Tut! talk of Greece, Rome, Europe! they are left
To moulder in the dust of Fogeydom.
We lack the time to read their epitaph.
Well, Europe is the tail-end of the past
And wags a little; but—oh pshaw! What's that?
It wags because we live to give it life.
    A. Given a sulky—short-time-horse—race course
        and
A fast young man—the dust is sure to fly.
We have them all, and dust enough to blind
Ourselves. A billion people will reduce
Our oats and—speed. We then shall learn, what now
We fail to see, that they who fastest run
Will soonest find the goal.
    B.   The present for
The present and the future for itself.
    N. The future cannot eat the bread we waste.

Then let us, while we dine, remember that
Posterity must sup off what we leave.

    B. Just so; and see how we develop things
And leave them handy for posterity.
It's wonderful; it's more than wonderful,
The way we get our railroads, boats, big farms—
Big everything to match the country's size;
And all by Uncle Samuel saying, Let
It be.

    N. More wonderful than wise; and yet
Not wonderfully wonderful. Who gets
The good of it?

    B.   Of course, the country.

    N.   Let
Us see. A railroad built. Ten millions paid
By government, the States and people on the route.
Five millions pay six thousand, who have built
The road, and five the half-a-dozen men
Who sat and played a game of euchre then
Gave word, Men, build that road. Which do you call
The country—The six thousand or the six?

    B. Undoubtedly, she gets the good of it.

    N. Yes, as she would if you and I should rob
The treasury and pay some men to take
Our plunder to a private place.

    B.   Well, there's
The road; and roads we certainly must have.

    N. In such a way? At such a price? Built for
Five million; costing ten. What get we for
The other five? Six lawful thieves. Dear sir!

'Tis so. Most these developments are schemes
For theft, and our developers desire
The country's progress as the horse thief does
That of the stolen animal he rides.
Few schemes of progress are on foot without
A thief upon their back; because we have
So many valuables lying loose.
Now take the road the country's money built.
The six who played the game have got it as
Their stakes; because they so developed things.
Henceforth there is a partnership in gain
Between the country and the mighty six;
These helping that and that the life of these.
The *country* means the millions, who divide
One half the good. Ths six divide the other half,
A glorious tribute this to equal rights!
No wonder that we have developers!
Take next your mammoth farm. Fertility
Exhausted by the mile, to feed a few
And make a millionaire; the country's fat
Glutting the markets of the world, that one
May be plethoric at the cost of all.
And profits minimized—but swelled
By acres to prodigious aggregates—
By which the toiler's profits minimize,
Who labors more and gets one tenth, or less;
Thus pinching millions by their "enterprise."
Alas the country that has such developers!
It is but dying of giganticide.
For what are these and other schemes of greed

But cups with which they draw the country's blood;
Our boasts, but pledges to posterity
To leave our gridiron and the country's bones?
Let us place Equity before us on
A pedestal; then bow, and on our knees
Ask why a few who have the cool and hard
Audacity of greed, and wizard skill,
Should thus be free to prey upon the wealth
That is the heritage of all, and use
The honest toiler as an instrument—
In the simplicity of pure intent—
To perpetrate this gross iniquity
And ignorantly play the suicide.
The oracle will be as marble, mute.
Development is incidental to
Their greed. Fraud is the great prime factor in
Affairs; for fraud it is, howe'er it gets,
That takes our wealth without equivalent.

    B. And yet we must develop, after all,
Or else die poor with millions 'neath our feet.

    N. Develop what? Not covert theft, but toil;
Not leagues of land, but character; not mines
So much as men, nor cliques as citizens.
Thus far we legislate the trickster up,
The toiler down. We give facilities
To Knavery in its craft, and fill the path
Of Industry with stumbling-blocks. We bend
The knee of sycophants to Genius—that
Is oft but pampered Indolence—and warp
Our nose at hands that touch the dirt. Yes sir,

We deify the drone that lives to eat
What others earn, and step on him who earns
What others eat.   So true is this, that we
Esteem those lowest whom we need the most,
Those highest whom we need the least.   Thus wealth
And social status grade from industry
To throne-hights of imperial laziness.
Who does the most is least.   Who does the least
Is most.   Thus industry is handicapped.
We need a gospel whose beatitudes
Are based on worth, as gauged by what
We do to meet the common wants.   The prime
And never ceasing wants of man are the
Imperative; and that which meets them must
Be deemed superlative.   Our dudish whims
And trumperies—the trifles of a day—
The jingling emptinesses that we drool
On, are as nothing to our mother's milk.

   B.   But brains deserve the highest market price.
Why, any mule has muscle.   It is brains
That wins.

   N.   Yes, wins, not earns.   Pray what is brains
As a commodity?   Must it be weighed
By pennyweights and valued by carats—
Each organ have its own specific price?
Then cry down muscle; let us be all brains
And dwell in castles made of air, be clothed
With sunshine and subsist on angels' food.
But while we still are muscle, flesh, and bone,
And get along in a material way,

Muscle will be a necessary thing;
Hence were it premature to cry it down.
Or give to brains preeminence, then grade
It in the bulk—by quality, not kind—
And cultivate the universal brains.
For why have muscle minus brains when we
Can have it plus? The germane blunder of
The ages shews right here—a blunder now
Become a petrified oppression and
A suicidal wrong. Muscle has been
Belittled, and degraded that it might
Be little, then denied its rights. Toil has
Been plebeianized, the toiler doomed, by scant
Reward, to be the crafty sluggard's drudge.
Who gives with greatest faithfulness his time,
His energies, his life, to aid the weal
Of all, is trodden down, and then condemned
For being down, and there, by arrogance
Of egotistic tyranny, is doomed
To stay, unless, by some herculean feat,
He smites the hydra of society
And gains a place with men.
  B.   You cannot mean
That all must share alike, incompetence
And indolence be deemed at par. Then were
There no incentives to excel.
  N.   I mean
The opposite. I mean, democracy
Within the realm of toil; that quantity
And quality—not aristocracy

Of kind—should be the guage of its reward.
I mean, that faithfulness in any branch
Should equalize the possibilities
In that with any other branch.   I mean,
That we should legislate to raise the poor.
Assume the abnormalty of their
Condition and restore them as we do
The sick.   Remove the pestilential cause
Of most their poverty and wretchedness—
The fumes that have the scent of brothel, blood,
And every poisonous stench in one—instead
Of leaving these for weakly natures to
Inhale, that barrel-paunches may distend.
Degrade no class by a degrading pay
For faithful work; but make it *possible*
For all to rise.   Trust not the wretch whom we
Have cursed with an adverse environment
To doom his child to dungeon ignorance.
In brief: restrain the rich and help the poor
To rise.   No prudent shepherd turns his flock
To feed upon the mow and leaves the goats
To waste what ought to feed the sheep.   Yet so
Have we.   And while the goats grow sleek, we stroke
Their backs and kick the sheep, whose wool must
         keep
Us warm.   And then we compliment ourselves;
Because the scrambler makes the fodder fly.

    SCENE.—*In the public hall.*

 NORTON.   My brothers! I esteem this office as
The highest place to which I could be called—

To shape their thought, and guide their action, who
Would recognize a *Human Brotherhood*.
Now, by the grace of friendship and your votes
Elected President, I shall proceed
To state my views—first of society
At large, its wrongs and rights, then how those
    wrongs
May be redressed, the rights secured. The past
Has been a worshiper of Power; nor is
The present free from that idolatry.
'Twas first the brawny force of brutish men;
And then the force of favored intellects;
And now of unrestricted wealth. And each
Of them has had its abject devotees.
The first made nations stagger as it strewed
The earth with skulls. The next, by cunning, yoked
Mens' minds with false philosophies of life
And made them beasts of burden to their peers.
The last—as ruthless as its ancestors—
Holds a hard hand upon our loaf
And makes us do obesiance for our slice.
Power may be Liberty's right arm. And such
It is when it insures our rights. But when
Infringing on the rights of others, it
Is despotism, gloze it as we may.
Ask, What is right? It is an equal chance
To share the common stock, by common toil,
And be protected by the common arm;—
For Dives no more; for Lazarus no less.
And now I ask, Have you an equal chance?

In view of all the facts I answer, No;
And thousand-throated laws of people yet
Unborn will emphasize that No. To have
Your children doomed to disability
Because of ignorance that is entailed
By ages of oppression, gives you not
An equal chance. To be entrammeled with
The prejudices of a social state
That darker days have fastened on you, gives
You not an equal chance. To have men look
On you as on a lower order and
To legislate you to a lower place,
Gives not an equal chance. To add your share
Unto the total of the nation's wealth,
Yet not receive in measure as you give,
Gives not an equal chance. To do a work
That more contributes to the country's needs,
And yet receive less pay than those who do
The less, gives not an equal chance. To make
It possible for an insatiate greed,
And expert cunning, to monopolize
Their rounded millions by their wits, gives not
An equal chance. To let the millionaire
Transmit his spoil to ravenous hands, gives not
An equal chance. To let these legatees
Employ their wealth as lever-power to gain
Them more, gives not an equal chance. In all
These ways you have been robbed, and are; robbed of
Your rights; robbed of the dearest elements
Of liberty.

Big Bill. That's so.

N. And here I state
An axiomatic, adamantine truth;
Whoe'er is privileged beyond ourselves
Has more than right or we have less. And power
Is privilege; and wealth is power; and who
Has wealth beyond his share is privileged
To be a despot; which is wrong. The rich
Will say that we have equal privilege
With them of getting wealth. I answer, 'Tis
Akin to savagery to make the land
A carcass and allow the strong to gorge
And starve the weak. I answer, Right is
Not the slave, it is the lord of Power. The power
To brain me gives to none the right. No more
Does power to rob. The power to take by force
The product of my toil gives none the right.
No more does power to take by artfulness;
Nor more the product of the country's toil.
We ask not such equality. We want
No partnership in wrong, but right. We make
The substance of our lives a common stock;
Then we demand the worth of what we pay.
We ask no more; and we protest against
The use of false keys by the more adroit.
But some expatiate on the rights of wealth.
That has no rights to which men have no right.
And such is wealth that multiplies their power.
And such is power from wealth that is not earned.
I ask, can much create the right to more?

I ask, is evidence of what is paid
But proof of what the country owes? I ask,
Must rich men melt their gold to manacles
And make us slaves, then wax sarcastic by
Reminding us of our equality?
Should wealth keep gathering in these focal hoards,
To what stupendous tyranny must their
Oppressions grow! We, relatively, should
Be serfs to those who held our loaf, ourselves.
Indeed, our syndicates are money-kings,
Whose millions rule the separate realms of wealth
And threaten us with iron sceptered wrongs.
They rob us from the cradle to the grave,
And squeeze our corpse in sepulture for blood.
We hear the claims of genius trumpeted,
Which, nineteen times in twenty, means but shirk.
But give us genius of the genuine kind.
What then? A pivot-fact is overlooked.
The product of the past—its brain and brawn—
Is common property, on which we all
Have equal claim. Who draws on this is so
Far debtor to the common fund and earns
But profit on the capital. But men
Have been so purblind to the fact that, when
One blinked the debt and claimed the principal,
The law allowed the fraud. He thus
Has been rewarded for the genius of
Our ancestors. As well reward one for
The railroads that the country's money built,
Because he made a better coupling for

Their cars.   But ask, Is genius such that he
Whose services are needed most deserves
The least?   Must one be priveleged to waste
And others doomed to want, because the first
Effeminates us while the other feeds ?
Is Nature's plan, a blessing for a few
And for the rest a curse, that genius is
So multiform?   And must their penalty
Be poverty whose genius craft taboos?
But why go further, like a ferrit, through
The burrows of their sophistry?   Brothers !
We are the footballs of the lords of power.
Booted with wealth, they kick us to and fro.
   Big Bill.   That's so.
   N.   We must assert the might of right,
As they the right of might, and rouse ourselves
To leave the graveclothes of the past, and in
A resurrected manhood stand upon
An equal level with the favored ones.
Yet understand me here.   While I denounce
Their lordly power, and breathe my protest, with
The utmost emphasis of soul, against
Their usurpations, I do not forget
That they have been, and are, supported by
The sanctions of the law.   And few of us,
'Tis probable, would spurn if offered us,
What they possess.
   B. B.   That's so.
   A Voice.   (*In an undertone.*)   Bill's right this
      time.

N.   The primal wrong, we see, is in the law.
Correct it, we correct resultant wrongs.
'Twere well to note that what is rooted in
The centuries cannot be uprooted in
A day.   Nor is it by a cyclone of
Revenge that we can serve ourselves.   To wreck
Our neighbor will not build us up.   What reared
The wrong, reversed, must tear it down.   But how
Can we reverse?   Prevent monopolies
Of land.   Our life is in it.   Let it be
For homes, not fortunes; for the many, not
The few.   Confine the working of our mines
Within the bounds of our necessities;
Nor let a dozen make us jackals, while
Their pockets hold the lion's share; yea, while
The country buys their surplus up, to save
It from decay and make them sleek.   In all
Its railroads let the State hold stock, to have
Its finger on their pulse; and let it press
The profits to the lowest point, to check
The growth of greed; nor let it millionize
A few.   Tax anacondic syndicates—
Which make the toiling citizens their prey—
Upon a rising plane.   They need a scotch
To make them ease their coils.   Our patent laws
Must be revised.   Let manufacturers
Compete on paying license for the right
And royalty on what they make—and so
Prevent the bloat of huge monopolies,
The breath of whose extortions blights the bloom

Of trade and turns a blessing to a curse.
And do not royalize the patentee
With royalty, giving a Morse or Howe
The crown that other hands had wrought, because
They added each a gem. Tax wealth upon
A sliding scale; for 'tis her wealth must meet
The country's bills; and they who hold it hold
It but in trust. Tax it when death ensues
From one to seventy-five per cent. By such
Devices we may part prevent, part cure,
This dropsy that is threatening us with death.
That such were just 'tis clear. 'Tis needful for
The general good; and on the good of all
Hangs that of each. The individual needs
Not what would keep a host; and hence
He wrongs a host in hoarding what they need.
And is not his: and aught that overmetes
His toil cannot be his. The dead has ceased
His wants, powers, rights; nor must we recognize
The ghost of his prerogative and let
Posthumous proxies have transmitted power
To scourge the living. Whence it came is where
His wealth belongs. In brief—the motto for
The coming time is this: *Who earns must have;
Nor more nor less than what he earns.* Towards this
The index finger of the present points;
Towards this the caravan of progress moves.
And now I say, Go on and agitate.
Make wings for truth and let her fly abroad.

(*On the street.*)

Bob Snag. What think you of our President?
He knows a thing or two.

Lew Lurk. His talk has too much twoness.

B. S. Why now, I thought he gave the sharks
slam-bang.

L. And who would fish without a bait? I've seen
These split-tongued gentlemen before to-day.
They talk on both sides of a fence at once.
Oh yes! Denounce the rich, to tickle us,
Then talk of righting things by law; as though
The villains didn't make the laws to suit
Themselves. I tell you, there's a crack in all
Such talk. But I'm not cracked enough to swallow it.
This waiting—having patience—letting things
Work out, means talk instead of do. But I've
A heap of faith in doing something, and
In doing it at once. Then see how slick
The way they made him President. They must
Have thrown their ropes and got the gang-plank out
Before he reached the dock. No time to speak
Or think before the thing was done. It's true
He knows a thing or two.

B. S. Well, anyway,
He's smart.

L. Yes, smart enough to make us smart.

(Scene—*The Detective's back room.*)

Detective. Has not your lady friend come with
you yet?

Dark Lantern. That theme was last and now
      is first with you.
   D.   I vow, Joblinsky, but you tantalize me
With your tardiness.   'Twere better not
To tell of Paradise than close the gates
Against my hopes.   Come, let me see
The only one that I have dared to love.
She must be an uncommon creature thus
To rapture me unseen.   Men say that mind
Can act on mind without regard to space.
And verily my soul is magnetized
By hers.   Tell me that I shall see her ere
Another sun is crimsoned in the west.
   D. L.   What more can you than love?   And that
      you say
You do.   What more can she than love?   And that
I say she does.   The proof is in your heart,
As you have said.   But I can tell you more.
Your love has seen your face and likes you well,
And calls you love, and says your kiss was sweet,
And that she hopes it was a drop of a
Full sea that she may drain.
   D.   Excuse me if
I play the fool, as every man does once.
But what was love has evoluted to
A passion, and I feel exalted, by
The law of differentiation, to
A higher type of being.   You, perhaps,
Have not attained to this, and cannot know
The scientific potency of love,

Whose furnace fires make more than trickles from
A cold heart's icicles, distilling light,
Etherial spirit in the heated still,
Which, for receiver, wants another heart.
Nay, surely, if this power had touched your heart,
Your pity would have wings for me.
    D. L.   What would
You have?
    D.   Herself, and blend our lives in one.
    D. L.   Sure as I know her heart that wish is hers.
But she would know how brave your love can be—
How much it dares—while she gives proof of hers.
Your love has made my lips the duct through which
The stream has flowed. Now dare you wed her as
You kissed? Her soul is so much like the rock
It dares. Dare yours? Or do you fear to trust
Her word?
    D.   Marry by proxy! Can the thing
Be done with all our fussy laws?
    D. L.   It can;
And she will hold to it and think you brave.
    D.   Tell me the way and I will find the will.
    D. L.   Use her true name with yours and I will
          play
The bride, clad in her dress and veil; and when
Your fates are one she scarce will give you time
To sigh ere you shall press her hand and lips
And call her yours.
    D.   I vow, but she is more
And more to me. But is your size so near

To hers that you could personate her to
The wearing of her dress?

    D. L.   As to the bust,
Mine might be hers.

    D.   Oh queenly fullness for
A woman's form! And length?

    D. L.   ·So near
You scarce would note a fault.

    D.   Suberb! Is she
Prepared to set the day?

    D. L.   She says that you
May choose the day.

    D.   Then why delay when that
But chafes the heart? How will to-marrow suit?

    D. L. Right well if that be what you choose.

    D.   • It is.

    D. L. Then ere the day be gone your eyes and lips
Shall meet, and you shall greet her as your wife.
But ere that comes I want to do one more
Great deed.

    D. Wipe out the depot for the boys?
Yes, let the vultures have their gizzards warmed.
I wish a red-hot shot were in their hearts.

    D. L. This night my eyes shall watch the perch and warm
Them all they want. The next good news that comes
To you shall have two wings.

    D.   Yes, love and fire;

And both alike make hotter still my heart.

SCENE—*In the Detective's Lodgings.*

DETECTIVE. I vow, but nature has outdone herself
In making you a manly man with all
Of woman's lovely qualities. It must
Be that she takes an evoluting step
In you, combining what is best in both.
You simulate the sex amazingly.
I might have wished you were a woman but
I recollect your word that she is not
Inferior to her representative.

    D. L. You soon shall have a chance to judge.

    D.   I'd risk
A thousand justices detecting you.
Here comes the justice. I will have my friends
Come in. (*Enter justice followed by two others, when the marriage ceremony is performed.*)

    D. (*In a whisper.*) Is she at hand?

    D. L.   Yes, when
These leave. (*Exeunt justice and others. Bell rings at the front door.*)

    D. That must be her.

    D. L.   Your wife is here.

    D. Oh, fortunate! You introduce her. But
There needs no ceremony in a case
Like this.

    D. L. Then none there shall be, for my name,
Which was Lille Slave, is now Lille Swab. Then
    see

Your wife in me. Yes, look; I am your wife.
(*Laughing.*)

D. What! you a woman? You Joblinsky! You Lille Slave? Are you in earnest now? Tell me.

D. L. You so will find; and may I give you joy!

D. Blessed deception! and more blest to be
Thus undeceived. Your words prove true, and more
Than true, in every syllable. I looked
For ruby and a diamond meets my eye.
Now there is double sweetness in your kiss.
(*Kisses her.*)

(*A knock at the room door. A man enters.*)

DETECTIVE ELLINWOOD. John Swab?

D. The same.

E. My name is Ellinwood. I called—
Ah! there's the very article I want,
Though in a somewhat curious looking wrapper.
You will come with me Joblinsky.

D. That is
My wife.

E. Perhaps. But don't you think it just
A trifle ticklish for a man to let
His wife be out at night playing with fire
About a railroad depot? Come along;
We understand the wife arrangement.

D. What—
What do you mean?

E. I mean that something mean
Was tried last night by one Joblinsky, and
Your *wife* knows what it was. But come along.

D.   Shew your authority for her arrest.

E.   For hers or his I have too much for health.
The why and wherefore will reveal itself
As soon as pleasant to the one concerned.
If you can take advice, I say, keep cool.

D.   I do protest against—

E.   I don't deny
The privilege. Go on protesting. But
We have to go another way.

D.   By all that's human! Do you mean to handcuff her?

E.   A bracelet; that is all.

D.   I swear, it is
Outrageous, fiendish, hellish, damnable!

E.   Why not
A woman wear the ornament she earns?

D. L.   Keep heart. My heart at least will be with you this night.

D.   O Liberty! O Justice! are
Your bones about the kennels of the tyrant? (*To Ellinwood.*)
A moment and I'll go with you.

E.   Come at
Your leisure; we may want you yet. (*Exeunt.*)

D.   Oh me!
Oh me! oh me! A married man without
A wife. My heart's one jewel seen then snatched
Away while I was gloating o'er my prize.
The cup of matrimonial bliss against
My lips then broken ere I taste. My life's

Trimmed wick ablaze and then blown out. My sun
Eclipsed at the horizon's verge. Oh the
Keen stinging of a venomed tongue, to hear
The fellow call my wife Joblinsky! Yes,
My wife—my wife! Why, what am I about?
The fool I am to let her go and I
Stay here. My wife in handcuffs! Rather let
My soul have handcuffs on it and he haled
To death in dark and loathsome dungeon. Then
To have him call my wife an article!
I wish I'd brought the claret from his nose
For that. Well, anyway, I'll follow her
And die in slow conjugal martyrdom.
But whitherto? What station-house? I am
Perplexed—perplexed. By Jupiter! affairs
Have got a most reversionary cast.
The moneron represents my State. One hour
The highest type of manhood's bliss is mine;
The next, inglorious proneness in the slime
Of a primordial woe.—The wretch, the fiend!
I wonder what was couched at back of that
Enigma, "We may want you yet." No doubt
It is a cloud that shadows forth a storm.
May want you—you—you; meaning me. I'll arm
Myself and make them pay for what they get.
I'll get two good revolvers, trusty friends—
Friends that will do my bidding—and a dirk,
Then die amid the trophies of revenge.—
May want you yet. The Parthian import of
That backward shot has struck a vital part;

Nor can I draw the arrow out.   There is
A density of meaning there that is
Too much for me.   (*A knock.*)   Oh that I had my
    arms!
Who's there?
   A Voice.   Bob Snag.
   D.   Come in. (*Enters.*)   You startled me.
Strange feelings visit men at times and, like
A swarm of vultures on a carcass, tear
Their heart as common carrion, and are hard
To drive away.   I was engaged in such
A task when—knock, I heard you at the door.
   B. S.   No wonder.   That's a warning sign to bid
You watch the nor'west corner of affairs
For squalls.   I've come to say that hell's cut loose
Our stays, and things are getting tangled up,
And we may all get beached, or something worse.
I heard a stranger whispering on the dock
About a dwarf who had some pantaloons
For sale the day that Boyle was killed.   He had
A mousing look, enough to give a chap
The cholera.   And sure enough it made
Me sick; and so I dropped my work to let
You know.   And now, if I know anything,
The thing for you to do is just to cast
Your shadow somewhere west of here or else
In Canada.   But if they should come up
With you, don't squeal.   You see, I've done the best
I can for you and hope you'll turn up trumps.
   (*The Detective groans.*)

What! waterlogged like that? Come, man your
    pumps
And luff and you'll come out all right. But hard
Your helm at once.
    D.   Thanks Bill. I want to be
Alone to lay my plans.
    B. S.   Good-by then. Best
Of luck. (*Exit. A long pause.*)
    D. That strands me quite. Henceforth I must
Be battered by the billows of misfortune.
Those liquid sharks will gnaw me, plank by plank,
Till not a vestige of the hulk remains.
Luck was it that he said—the best of luck?
The best of luck is his whose death was an
Eternity before his birth. Death—life.
They are the ventricles of Nature's heart,
Which keep the venous and arterial blood
In ebb and flow of rushing consciousness.
But who shall give us their anatomy?
Who tell us all the mystery of their tides?
Is every life a tide-rush through her heart,
To be repeated in another life,
And each evolving towards a higher mark?
I am dumbfounded and agnosticised
In presence of such problems. But enough.
To live is but to be a fool. To die is—well,
No worse. And yet there is a clamminess
About this thought of death that fidgets one.—
Was that a knock? No. Only a coal-cart.
What can I hope? Despair! hold thou my fate.

No, that were hardly worthy of myself.
I'll flee to Canada and leave them in
The lurch. And yet, who knows how near they
    are?
They may be coming up the street. But if
I went to Canada, what then? Must I
Leave all behind, save what I fain would leave;
Live like a felon in a chosen cell,
Startled at every step about the door;
Yearning to know, and yet afraid to hear,
Of things behind? That could but be the dregs
Of life—a prolongation of the pangs
Of death, whose torment every year would still
Increase. But who knows where the tyrants are?
Oh, that I had my arms to meet the worst!
Then would I rid the world of one of them.
Enough; I have the matter in my hands.
By this I cheat them if I cannot kill. (*Taking a
    vial from a drawer.*)
Here's everything between a thumb and finger.
                    (*Holding up the vial.*)
There are two worlds—one on each side of it.
Inside is death; outside is life—here time,
Which makes me what I am, and there
Eternity, which makes me what I was
Before I was. I am the god of Fate
And hold his keys as master of myself.
I will defy them to their worst and leave
Them but a shell. So shall they see that I
Was much too great for them, and brave as great.

(*The front door bell rings.*) By Jupiter! I wonder
    whether that be them.
(*He drinks.*) That settles it. Now let them come.
(*A pause.*) Not them? I was precipitate. I might
Have waited and consulted further with
Myself. But it is done and cannot be
Undone. Oh me! oh me! I was too rash.
I wonder whether it is still too late
To get assistance. No, that scarce would do.
It may be I shall come out right. Indeed,
I feel as though a sleep would pull me through.
It will refresh me and compose my nerves.
                      (*He sleeps and dies.*)

(SCENE—*The same. Detective Trip at the door.*)

    TRIP. (*To landlord.*) Is this Swab's room?
    LANDLORD. (*Whispering.*) Yes, he was married
        there
An hour ago and got his honeymoon
Eclipsed without the first forewarning from
The almanac—went out like spitting on
A·spark. Detective took her off and had
The wristlets on her. Something's up.
    T.   There may
Be more than one thing up. Swab, I suppose,
Went with her?
    L.   No, I reckon not. I heard
Him in his room a little while ago. (*Trip looks
    through the keyhole.*)

T. There's some one lying there upon the lounge.
(*They knock loudly.*)
L. That must be him.
T. He remains there still.
Have you a chair at hand?
(*Looks through the transom.*)
There's something strange
About his looks; he might be dead.
L. Here, I've
A key. (*They enter.*)
T. Yes sir; dead enough, dead enough. He'll tell
No tales. That puts the brakes on us.
SLIM SAM. (*Stepping up behind.*) Why, is
The detective dead?
T. Why do you call him
The detective?
S. S. Why—well, it is a name
We had for him; that's all.
T. Names, sometimes, are
Geographies of men, and indicate
Their latitude and longitude, and tell
The climate, soil, productions. Sometimes they
Are histories in themselves, which, rightly read,
Would tell us things we have most need to know.
Why man! what makes you look so bad—as though
You'd lived a month on cucumbers and krout.
S. S. I'm not a-feeling well. I reckon it's
Through finding of him dead has done it.
T. Ah!
You seem to take great interest in his case.

A longshoreman ain't you?

S. S.   Well, yes.

T.   I guess the shakes are coming on you. Hold
Your bones together lest they scatter and
We have to pick you up in pieces. Say,
Did you ever see this Swab about the
Levees? What! bad as that? Well, the landlord's
Sent to get the coroner, and he can look
On two of you at once. You take the thing
To heart uncommonly. I guess you know
So much it makes your stomach trouble you.
What! worse and worse? Well now, see here—I
       was
But chaffing you. But serious now. What *do*
You know about this Swab?

S. S.   A sight too much,
I swear. But I must go.

T.   Don't hurry. Did
You see him any time the day that Boyle
Was killed?

S. S.   I have to go.

T.   See here now. Tell
Me what you know about the Boyle affair
And I will make it worth your while. Come now.
There's cash behind this thing and it is bound
To come.

S. S.   You can't prove anything by me. (*Exit.*)

T.   There seems to be the scent of something
      there. (*Aside.*)

SCENE—*On the Street and in the Hall.*
LEW LURK.   What think you of this Norton?
BLACK JOE.   He is smart—
Sharp as red pepper.   Seems to know the lie
      of things and what we need.
Yes, smart enough.
  L.   And all the worse for that if we don't get
The good of it.
  B. J.   He starts off like a brick.
  L.   Of course; I don't say but he does.   And who
Would not, as strumpets rouge their faces, have
His frontispiece look fair, to gain his ends,
When there is rottenness and death behind?
  B. J.   His ends?   Why, what do you suspect
      him of?
  L.   Oh! That's too much to say.   I don't suspect
Him in the least.   My finger could not touch
An overt act of wrong.   I could not give
A name to anything that seems amiss
More than I can tell you what a bad smell
Looks like.   The things that smell are those that men
Conceal.   The graveyard motives buried in
The breast, which have the scent of death—we see
Not these; and oft we only know the place
Of their interment by the flowers above
Them.   Yet, in Norton's case, I but suggest
The possible.   *If* he should be a black
Sheep, all the worse for being smart.
  B. J.   And all
The better if he aint.

L. Yes, *if*.

B. J. Well, now,
What's up that you are smelling after him
This way? I'd like to know and watch the cub
If anything is wrong.

L. Nothing, I say,
That's nameable; but—well, you know it pays
To keep an eye on the barometer;
Especially when fellows with their pile
Have taffy talk for working men like us.

B. J. The sweetest taffy in a case like this
Is unadulterated truth; and he
Let out a heap of it.

L. Exactly so.
Does it not take a coating of the truth
To fit an error for the palate? Who
Would take a pill if he must suck it down?
Recall the way he hemmed and hawed about
Obeying law; about forbearance towards
The rich, and such like stuff. Of course, he said
The laws are wrong, the rich are knaves, and all
The rest. Then why not put the rich astride
The law and blow them both to smithereens?
That looked too tarnal like a snake's tail to
Be laughed about. The other end may not
Afford the safest sport. (*Bob Snag coming up.*)

Bob Snag. Going to the
Hall, eh?

L. Yes, Joe and I are on the way.

B. S.   Well Lew, I've made a quid of what you
          said
To me the other night and think you're less
Than fifty yards of right.   But I'd not thought
Of it enough to ask a countersign.
    L.   Now, Bob, you watch his words—especially
The ones that hitch in coming out, for which
The half inclines to make apology.
    Dig down into their undermeaning and
You'll find a rat.   Now make a note of this:
He wont ask fellows such as you and I
To hold an office ; not a bit of it.
    B. S.   I have no hankering after one.
    L.   No more
Have I.   But there's a principle at stake
In this—a vital principle, and one
We need to guard.   We are a Brotherhood
Of working men, while he has capital
And cannot be in sympathy with us.
I know that I could fill the office that
He holds, and better represent our class.
Not, as I said, that I am wanting it.
I only say that he is not the man ;
And men like you and I will have no show,
Except to pay the fiddler while he plays.
Just think of organizing to protect
The working man, and making Capital
Our president!
    B. S.   I hadn't thought of that.
    L.   The outside of a thing is all that most

Men see. But schemers keep a lock and key
Upon their real selves; and only through
The keyhole of their cunning speech can we
Look in and see them as they are. But here's
The hall. I guess we'll have a crowd to-night.

(*They enter. After preliminaries Norton addresses the Brotherhood.*)

NORTON. My brothers! I invite attention to
My former theme. Lend me your judgment and
Your confidence. Let prejudice be still
And reason rule. So shall we find the truth.
Already I have partly pointed out
The inequalities in power possessed
By rich and poor, which leave the latter an
Unequal chance to rise. I hold, that He
Who made us wisely gave diversity
Of genius, that its aggregate might meet
The wants of all and all their wants. In one,
We see Imagination wave her wand,
When myriad phantasies have concrete form.
Another notes the germed utilities
In nature's seed and bids the lobes expand.
Another puts his hand upon a crank
And guides the forces others first evoked.
And still another has the thewey force,
That executes the plans his fellow thought.
Thus each has aptitudes that, unrestrained,
Will gravitate to their appropriate sphere.
The heresy of our economy
Has classified this genius as the high

And low, and says, that equal faithfulness
Must have unequal pay. If classify
We must, count first the first in ministry
To human wants—such ministry as will
Be needed while the race endures. But break
The cordon-codes whose selfishness engirds
The few and leaves the rest to poverty.
Crown genius in the genius of the age,
Whose reach is toward equality.
Allowing for preparatory toil
And other cost, gauge pay by quantity
And quality of work, not kind. It slaps
Our Reason in the face to say, that what
Is healthy leisure merits more reward
Than what benumbs the body with its wear.
Thus far I have your heads and hearts. Now come,
And I will trace this principle as it
Concerns ourselves upon another side.
The welfare of society demands
That all shall have an ample chance to rise.
And this is man's inalienable right.
No calling needful to our wants can we
Afford to relegate to poverty,
To grangrene on the body corporate.
Much less must we degrade whom most we need.
Your judgment will assent as 'twixt yourselves
And those above you. Now apply the square
The other way. And first, I want to ask,
How many want to farm?

  Several voices.   Why none.

N.   And why?
A voice. Big work and little pay.
N.   You hit the mark.
Now make a note. The farmers constitute
Two-thirds the toiling class; and hence two-thirds
The toilers have big work and little pay—
Such work and pay that you would shrink from it.
Yet what more honorable work than theirs,
Since necessary as the air we breathe?
The palmiest days of old saw statesmen at
The plow; and it would honor them no less
To-day, in spite of dudish dignity,
Which dreads the touch of common dirt. Then let
Us not imprint on it a brand of shame.
The pampered brand all toil, and we protest.
Shall we brand part, and not that part protest?
What! scrimp two-thirds, whose toil is hard as ours,
Then snub them on the ground that they are scrimped?
We could not burn a deeper brand into
The brow of toil. Better we hang ourselves
Than sink 'neath such a load of infamy!—
Now when I speak of equal rights I want
My words to have the largest latitude;—
Not only equal rights for You and I
With those above, but those below with you
And I. Not only have the rich no right
To an unequal share of what belongs
To all, ourselves have no more right. Yet here
Two-thirds the toilers are so poorly paid
That we would call it a calamity

. To share their lot. Thus do we own their lot,
Compared with ours, to be calamitous.
The voice of justice is against us here,
This equal work deserves an equal pay.
Then here's the sore where first to smear our salve
And do the justice that ourselves demand.
Here is the beck of opportunity
To give political economy
A trend towards justice, and to prove ourselves
Magnanimous. So may we arm our claims
On others with effectual power. And here
The difference shews between the giving and
The taking of a dose. But let us face
The remedy we recommend. Now ask
The possible. The farmer sells upon
The basis of a foreign price, and thus
Competes with foreign underpay, our arm
Too short to help on foreign soil. Help must
Be here at home, if help there be. Drive home
And clinch that fact. Note next,—he buys two-thirds
Of what we make, hence pays two-thirds of what
We get. As we environ those who sell
Against competitive assault we give
Extortion opportunity to squeeze—
An opportunity 'tis neither dull
To see nor slow to seize. Two-thirds of this
He bears, and we ourselves the rest. A part
Of this we take in what we get o'er what
We give for equal toil. Then as for us—
If justice guide our course—we must ourselves

Demand less pay or give him more; like him,
Compete with all the world, or he, with us,
Be walled against the world. Aught less than this
Is inequality, and so unjust.
How then shall we begin to equalize?
By raising at the bottom as we may
And lowering at the top. But little 'tis
That we can raise. Then climb the apex and
Begin to dock. And here 'tis pertinent
To catechise. Has this class special needs
That claim three dollars to the other one.
To house, feed, clothe, and educate itself?
If not, why treble pay for equal work?
Or double pay for what exhausts no more?
Or greater pay for less amount of toil?
Society has common needs, which ask
That they who wallow in the mire shall be
Upraised, to help where now they hinder all.
These needs are overlooked while we maintain
Mechanic aristocracy, and in
The trades have titular disparity,
From tailor knights to shears-armed baronets,
From brakeman earls to ducal engineers;
Whose pay is as their rank, while others do
The equal work and get the lesser wage
Of serfs. The favored ones are castled in
Their priveleges, walled and moated round
With prohibitions, while themselves would guard
The bridge to keep intruders out. Is this
Equality? Is this fair play? With such

Anomolies how can we better things? (*Murmers*.)
Yes yes. I know 'tis easier cutting out
Our neighbor's cancer than our own. But right
Is right whoever has to wince. It is
The truth that gives the knife its edge. 'Tis clear
The welfare of the great two-thirds deserves—
As it demands—our thought; and for its sake
And ours it must not be denied. Then view
This subject on the broadest plain. If we
Demur to dock the highest wage, what say
We that the lowest foots two-thirds the bill?
Can that be right? By no arithmetic
Can it be figured as equality.
At times we think our highest duty is
To strike for greater pay and fewer hours—
Which is equivalent to greater pay—
And thus draw further on their pocketbook.
If that be right, then I am blind to right.
The operations of the laws of trade
Admonish us. We need hydraulic force
To keep it up; because our level is
Above surrounding surfaces. We thus
Exhaust ourselves—and shall, till nature has
Its way; for wrong will prove re-active and
Retaliate in pay or penalty.
We have refused the pay, and get some small
Installments of the penalty; nor will
She fail to take the final cent. How this
Has been, and how it will be if we still
Persist, there needs no second-sight to see.

Discriminations favoring lordish trades
Attract the injured to the barbecue,
Of whom so many have already come
That they have left us little but the bones.
Nor will this cease until the wrong shall cease.

(*Murmers.*)

Murmer we may; yet, know ye all, it is
Not me is murmered at, but fate.   Persist
We may, but it will end as if one should
Present his nose to split a thunderbolt.
Our immigrants send down the murcury
In our thermometer and indicate
That we shall find it cold enough, ere long,
To freeze us into proverty, and drive,
Perhaps, to anarchy, which is mad death.
This or a levelling in wage is our
Alternative.   Thus much as 'twixt ourselves.
Next bring the screw on our extortioners—
To whose magnetic fingers sticks so large
A part of what they touch—by opening wide
Our gates of commerce to the world.   Shut up
Within ourselves we live upon ourselves
And find the diet weak.   And futhermore.   Prevent
The man whose pocketbook proclaims that he
Has now beyond his dues, depleting us
Still further, by manipulation of
The product of a thousand hands, to build
Himself a yellow monument and leave
To us the curse of his impoverishing.
In short, give equal opportunity

To all, in any calling, to ascend,
By industry. and that alone, the steps
That lead to competence. Again I say;
Equality in opportunity,
And opportunity within the bounds
Of right.

    ED. PRATT, SECRETARY. Now, through the kindness of your friend,
The President, our members who were in
The recent strikes may come to me and draw
Ten dollars each. For though he disapproves
Of strikes, the strikers have his sympathy.

    SCENE.—*On the Street.*

    LEW LURK. What think you now of Mr. President?
Our noble President?

    BOB SNAG.   There is enough
Of sense to color what he says and make
It look all fair. And yet—

    LURK.   Yes, I should say
And yet; and fifty yets before I gave
Consent to wittle wages down as he
Proposed. The boys won't swallow that. Once let
Him get that eel's tail through his hole and soon
The head will follow; bet your last red cent
On that. I tell you, he has too much craft
For us to trust his speech. It pays to watch
The man who smiles so unctiously, and while
He slobbers over us so feelingly,
Is only feeling for our pocketbook.

BLACK JOE. He shelled the dollars out, which
    hardly looks
Like craft or selfishness.
    L.   No fool could play
So smart a game; nor would a honest man.
Nature is nature, and she shews herself
The same at all times. Now, no man invests
Without expecting an increased return.
Hence, when you find one over-liberal, 'tis
But Arab hospitality which gives
To gain. His prodigality plays blab
On him. Free bait to-day; to-morrow, hook
And line. Who knows where all this money comes
From? Grant that he is not without his pile,
He would not use his own in such a way.
I wouldn't want to swear that he is not
The lickspit of the tyrants who would grind
Our noses off and kick us then because
We had no nose.
    B. J.   Do you suppose he is?
Could I think so, I'd want to bring him up
As sudden as the snapper of a whip
And make him crack a warning to the rest.
    L. Do you suppose that half of him could be
So smart and what remains a fool? Trust him
For knowing what a dollar's made for. He
Imagines we are fools. Perhaps we are;
But count me out sir, if you please. You can't
Blind Lew by throwing dollars round like dirt.
I've seen such tricks before to-day.

B. S.   You see
Beyond your nose; and that is more than most
Of us can say. We've been such tarnal fools
They just know how to work us.
    L.   You are right
They do. And they can always find some tool
That has a swivel-tongue, to talk all ways •
And use soft sawder, and to rosin us
With X's that will make it stick. And then
How good we are! So good that he could gulp us
        down,
Like oysters off the shell, and smack his lips.
But I for one don't relish being gulped,
Nor—gulled. How tenderly he touched on strikes,
Stepping with soft palaver round the theme,
As when a cat is creeping towards a bird!
But no palaver when he touched our pay.
Then he could rake us fore and aft and clear
The deck. And why? He let his heart loose then;
That's why. Now what's the English of it all?
Just this: don't blame the bosses, but yourselves,
For poverty. Its a confounded lie—
An everlastingly confounded lie!
    B. S. By thunder! but you've knocked the
        faucet out
Of him. We'll have to fix his pie.
    L.   I knew
You'd come out right when once you saw the point.
Of course, you judged him by yourselves and gave
Him credit for a good intent. But that

Don't do in such a crooked world as this.
I tell you, there are lots of men would grind
Their fellows into sausage-meat and sell
Them by the pound; and so, when that's the game,
I try to find a trump. What say you to
A meeting in my shop to-morrow night,
To talk of things and lay our plans?

    B. S.   A good
Idea that; I'm in with all my heart and soul.

    B. J. My shadow won't be far off when you
        meet;
For my name aint Joe Shirk.

    L.   That's true of both
Of you. Well, good-night boys. (*Exit Lurk.*)

    B. J.   Its lucky the
Detective died the time he did. That let's
Us out.

    B. S. As slick as if we'd greased the thing.
I guess we'll have to bake this fellow's beans;
But in a dish that won't be apt to leak.
Lurk, may-be, has a plan.

    B. J.   Suppose we get
Big Bill again to take a hand.

    B. S.   All right;
Bill's always sweet on such a job as this. (*Exeunt.*)

    SCENE—*In Lurk's Workshop.*

    LURK. Good deeds need no apology; and none
Are better than to put a nightcap on
A traitor that will put him fast asleep.

And where is traitor viler than the wretch
Who comes with crafty speech to counterfeit
A friendship that is but a mask for deeds
That stab our interests in a vital spot?
This craft needs answering with a quietus.
Such men are dangerous in proportion to
Their skill in hiding their designs. And such
Is his, that even you were fooled by him
Until I pricked the bladder, letting out
The wind of his pretence. You know as well
As I do that it isn't every fool
Can take you by the nose and bridle you.
But he did. Then consider what success
He must be having with the rest, who sat
With open mouth and took, like public sewers,
Whate'er he gave. My blood half freezes at
The thought, and all my feelings rouse to strike
In my defence and yours; for every man
Who earns his daily bread has here his life
At stake. His very life, I say; for he
Who takes our bread takes life; and he deserves
To forfeit what he aims to take.

 Big Bill.   That's so.

 L. Well, are you ready for a quiet job
That takes a grain of grit?

 Bob Snag.   A dozen grains
Are waiting for the word. Grit is the stuff
That makes the bones of men like us. We are
No chicken-livered cubs when treason shakes
Its red rag in our face. You beat the brush

And we'll bring down the game.
>   BLACK JOE.   Yes, you've thought out
The thing.   Set up your tenpins and we'll knock
'Em down.   There's satisfaction in a game
Like this—to slap the gay mosquito while
He sings.
>   B. B.   That's so.
>   L.   Three things are needed.   First,
Know where to find him at a certain time;
Next, how to fix him that the job will stay;
Then take our places and perform our parts.
>   B. S.   You see the points.   Now tell the moves
>   to make
And see who checkmates then.
>   L.   When next we meet
Will be the time to strike; and he must be
Alone.   When meeting closes, you get out
And double-quick it to the alley near
To Milligan's saloon and pick your spot.
I'll manage to secure his company,
And then accompany him within a block
Of where you are and leave him to proceed
Alone.   You know him by his ulster and
His hurried gait.   Now see how this will work:
When something happens him I won't be there.
And you, since members of the order, will
Be innocent as pumpkin pie and play
The crocodile.   Besides, the boys will all
Have seen you at the meeting, making you
Secure 'gainst spectacled suspicion as

A dead dog is against the whooping cough.
Well that's the plan; so when he comes along,
Of course you'll make the most you can of luck.

  B. S. You turn him loose and leave the rest to us,
We'll cure his corns that they will twinge no more.
Then let him try his scurvy tricks on us. (*The latch
     lifts.*)

  L. Sh—! I wonder who that is. Come in.
     (*Enter Slim Sam.*)

  SLIM SAM. Hello! a little squad. I thought from
     what
Your wife said you might be alone at work.

  L. I was until the boys came dropping in
Like you. I have a little job to do
On time. What's the good word?

  S. S.   The best I know
Is what we got last night.

  L.   So that you think
Was good?

  S. S. I thought it sounded more like sense
Than anything I've heard this many a day.
A cabbage heart grow tender—like fall rains.
Yes, Norton's good as ice in summer—good
To cool one's soul. Most Xtra Xcellent!
I guess we'll have him canonized Saint X.

     SCENE—*In Norton's private room.*

  GILLESPIE. I fear those murmers were the mut-
     terings of
A storm.

  NORTON. Then let it come, if come it must,

And clear the atmosphere.
    G.   They see us through
A mist and fear to follow where we lead,
As though our steps were o'er a quivering bog.
    N.   This is the crisis in the battle when
To falter were to fail.   Better at such
A time the followers than the leaders fear.
Courage is always mightiest at the front.
We look for stragglers in the rear.
    G.   ·   I fear
That most are much too far behind to feel
The forward impetus.
    N.   By so much are
We more than hangers-on.   Progress demands
High courage, both in leader and the led.
He penetrates the denser mists with his
Prophetic eye, and through their swathing folds
Perceives the landscape's mantled ghost, with here
A meadow, there a mountain, in a dim
Immensity; and so he travels on.
It is not his to ask how many form
The rear, nor to turn round to see how long
His shadow is.   Nor is it theirs to ask
How far he his before; but, dare they trust
The casting of his eye; and if they dare,
Then forward! march.
    G.   An ideal argument.
But neither see they, trust, nor seem inclined
To march.   They underestimate your worth
And work.   And so their ears are down to balk

If not to kick.
    N.   The wise are brave ; and brave
Men dare the underestimation of
Their fellows, knowing well that Time attends
On Justice and assigns to every man
His level at the last ; and better to
Be leveled up than down. Of course, men curse
The prophet ere they build his monument.
But let them curse; the monument will come.
Thousands have braved a thousand times as much
As we to win an epaulet. Then we
Can scarce afford to quail before a crowd
That may to-morrow shoulder us about—
We who may have our honors high emblazed
Among the 'scutcheons in the halls of time.
Our names made hallowed by the lapse of years.
    G.   We can't afford to venture much for Fame.
She has a most uncertain capital,
Which brings us but starvation dividends.
    N. A fillip for your fame. Yet I confess
That I would merit fame. And should I more,
I ask for Fame's attest to faithfulness.
Young Hotblood courts her at the cannon's mouth,
And, if she smiles, gives half his limbs and counts
The bargain cheap. Shall we dare less who strive
For more? the broad horizon of whose aims
Is in infinity. Great motives ought to have
The stronger grasp.
    G.   As true as law
And gospel in a quintessence. But we

Are called to deal with wills—or wonts. Admit,
The less they will to learn the more they need.
Still, who shall put the bridle on their will?
Let me suggest, that by a shaking up
Of oats, whose noise declares their scantiness,
We toll them after us. The noise would draw
From further than a bin of oats. In this
Way compromise between our conscience and
Necessity.

   N. The compromises that
Are hostages of cowardice are not
Begotten of our noblest hours. Yet would I shun
Antipodal extremes and sacrifice
Whate'er might merely minister to pride;
Whate'er would seem to have a tang of self;
Yea, and whate'er is but the drapery of
The truth. But let the virgin Truth be nude
I shall not shrink to shield her purity,
Nor to proclaim her virtues to the world.

   G. Gallant! But they see not her nudity.
They see her cast-off clothes and think her there.

   N. I cannot stop to doff my hat each time
A cricket chirps, nor to explain myself
To every beggar when I sneeze. The poor
Old world is sick—by far too sick for us
To shilly-shally with her case, which needs
Heroic treatment; and the doctor, not
The patient, must prescribe. (And here I need
No prudish modesty). I think I see
A remedy, and I prescribe, knowing

That she will gag before she gulps the dose.
But her extremity will open yet
Her mouth and let it go. I may not see
It done ; and she may e'en forget who left
The remedy. Such is the frostwork used
In building up a monument of fame.
Bright as 'twere solid sunlight, it dissolves.
And that which glitters most may be the first
To disappear. So cheap, one line has crowned
A Payne with bays; so dear, a Sophocles
Is half forgot. To me it matters not.
I fill my place in life's great drama and
Perform the part that Providence assigns.
I want my record writ in human lives ;
So shall it live when marble turns to dust.

    G. My sole concern is, how to write it there.
I lack your bold audacity of faith,
Which in the darkness firmly plants its foot,
Expecting solid rock.

    N.   We can afford
To dare while backed by the Omnipotent.
Look through His eyes, rely upon His arm
And go ahead.

    G.   Easy, no doubt, it is
To one who has the faculty of faith ;
But my more prying nature wants to see.

    N. Then shut your eyes and you shall see the
        more,
By shutting out the world.

    G.   Would we might live

To shake hands with the coming time, which Faith
Upon your watch tower sees approaching o'er
The plain.
   N. I doubt not thousands in the past
Have longed to see the day we see; and in
Our wished for day men still will wish to reach
An ideal that is ever on the move.
So will our human finity go on
To find the suburbs of infinity,
And spend, perhaps, eternity in quest.
This is the spur to life's activities.
In this, humanity is e'er a boy,
Strutting and stretching to become a man.
Be this our satisfaction, that we are
As cogs in the great wheel that grinds events,
And let us lubricate our energies.
When next we meet I mean to close
The statement of my views; and after that
We must proceed to spread ourselves abroad
And sow the country with our principles.
      Scene—*In the Public Hall.*
   Norton. Brothers, I now shall finish my remarks
Upon the subject of the former nights.
But first, I wish to touch some pustules that
Have been unseen, and which, when touched, may
    make
Us wince. Now see the inutility
Of strikes. They make you fight unarmed 'gainst
    those
In mail. Nay, men of millions quaff their wine

And make a strike a means of fleecing you
Still more, while smiling at the impotence
Whose fists are smiting adamant. But would
You probe this pustule to its core? Ask why
These constant feuds. Is not the gauntlet thrown
By those who have the highest wage, and so
The least occasion to complain? You must
Confess that this is so. Then why the strikes?
Because the bloated wage attracts the crowd
Till they are threatened by competetors,
'Gainst whom they raise their "union" barricades;
But which employers try to batter down,
While hungry thousands try to scramble o'er.
The level water needs no dam to keep
A fraction of its surface in its place.
No more the toilers where a level of
Equality prevails. There are no strikes
Amongst the great two-thirds that wants the men
Whose toes have scraped your heels. Now crack
    that nut
And find a kernel there.—While I declare
That I would rather be a flea upon
A dead dog than to live the life of some
Rich men, I cannot shut my eyes to facts.
I see that tyrants are not always rich.
I see the desperate and despotic means
Employed by wage-monopolists, to push
Up wages with discriminating force.
I see that those who get the ducal pay
Have ducal longings that destroy content—

An itching after more than what they need;
An envious wish to waste as others waste:
And hence, as lilliputian millionaires,
They shew the scurvy of improvidence. (*Murmers*).
Nay, do not murmur at the truth. If it
Has hurt you, take the hint and step aside.
A thunderbolt hurts only those who cross
Its path. I fear that most are squandering what
Might shelter from life's autumn rains; else why
So many liquor-dens, where capital
Is fattening on the poor? Thousands of these—
The bloated tyrants, whom the poor support
In their luxurious laziness—give back
A curse for all it takes to round their paunch.
And yet they strut on half the corners of
The streets. What better were you off should all
Have double wage and all *you* got but fill
Them up with lard? No no. Not what we get
Enriches us, but what we do not waste.
But could we all be rich we all would still
Be poor; as elephants were small as mice
Were mice the size of elephants. E'en now
You are not poor, save as your eyes turn up.
Look down and all are rich.—I now proceed
To sweep the wide horizon of the world,
In all the scope of mutual human rights.
And here I scout the mouldy arguments
Whose logic leans upon the obsolete
And keeps its dead eye fixed upon the past.
A living present needs providing for—

Not with the milk that served our infancy,
But with the meat that manhood masticates.
Then let us clear our eyes of selfishness
And look our present problems in the face.
The man most worthy of the name of man
Is he whose aim o'ermantles most with its
Beneficence. Indeed, the sainthood of
Our nature is the sympathy with man
Whose ardent outreach clasps its fingers round
The final volume of his destiny.
The preface and the introduction of
The race are written. Now the body of
The book remains to fill. The way in which
We write our page will shape the argument.
The man whose life revolves within himself,
Sucking, like autumn eddies in the woods,
The world's dead leaves of lucre to his heart,
Is but a fly-speck on the present page.
And nations with this sordid animus
Are blots. To have a better horoscope,
We need to view the world with other eyes
Than did our fathers. We must not regard
It as a chessboard, and the nations pawns,
For castles, bishops, knights and queen to move
Upon, until some Greatgrab checks. Instead,
They are as parts of one great city, where
Is a community of interests; where
There ought to be no slums, to serve the rich
As waste-bins, into which to cram the poor,
As garbage from their overloaded store.

Oceans have shrunk until they are but squares,
And channels streets, and islands neighbors, which
Can call and answer from each other's door.
And each decade will find them nearer still.
Then view the rights of man as more than ours—
Their scope as girting all the world; and deem
The duties of the nations as of man
To man. Twixt one or billions right is right.
You know the rights belonging to your trade?
You know the rights belonging to the rest.
You know the rights belonging to all toil.
You know the nation's rights. You know the world's.
Be jealous then for others' rights as yours;
For the revolving ages unify
The interests of the whole. Give to the world
The rights of intercourse, as you yourselves
Would jostle in the markets of the world.
Fear not destructive competition. That
You have. "Protection" guards our capital
From competition with the world, and so
The competion is twixt capital .
And poverty at home; and capital
Is king and has you in its gripe. Fling wide
The nation's doors. Let capital compete
With capital and bring its profits to
The common mean. But here you wince
And tremble for your wage. But if you fear
Equality, then take not Justice' name
In vain. Or fear you to compete—your choice
Is prisoner to necessity. You must. You can

But choose the spot on which the lever
Shall be placed—in Europe or at home.
Shut in your trade and hibernate—the swarms
Of Europe, driven before the whip of their
Necessities, will come and share your loaf.
Think of the great two-thirds that now competes
With Europe's poorest paid, in spite of sharks
That are protected in monopoly
At home, then answer whether you could not
Compete with those who get the highest wage,
Were this protection taken from the sharks.
But note : A less per cent. of wage is in
Our wares than those of foreign make. By so
Much more the purchaser is fleeced by him
That sells. So capital increases still
Its bloat. Hence 'tis not wage but greed that gets
Protection from the foreign price. Thus 'tis,
Whichever way we turn, we feel our gun's
Recoil. Our greed is crushing us. The blood
Already oozes from our pores—and will,
Till Reason rules and Justice gets her dues.
But what is Reason, Justice what? The rights
Of man as·man. With us, equality
In ultimates of wage, and values based
Upon per cent. of toil. With capital,
Close competition in the widest field.
With nations, recognition of the race
As one. The ideal of political
Economy is there, and a freed world
Shall wear that chaplet in the diamond age

To be; which will be when we rise to the
High eminence from which our reason and
Our sympathies shall view the world, and see
Our interests welded in a chain whose links
Depend upon the whole. And when we trust
That chain to hold our destinies, we all
Shall recognize THE HUMAN BROTHERHOOD,
Which God ordained, but man has erst ignored.
  (*The audience dispersing*).
  LURK. I compliment you, Mr. President,
For opening out so vast a vista to
Our view, and thus alluring onward, with
The prospect of the better time. Our aims,
As you present them, are the grandest, and
Well worthy of the most exalted minds.
Only Columbuses would dare so vast
An ocean, whose far continent mankind
Have been too dull to dream of, as they still
Dream on unconscious of the wakeful world.
But, some day, they will rub their eyes to learn
That we have found a world.
  N.   Exactly so.
The fundamental principles of right,
Twixt which and modern life an ocean lies,
Are yet, to most, an unknown continent.
Even ourselves scarce touch the mainland of
The rights of man as others will. Nor need
We till the islands are explored. But we
Are in the vicinage of vaster things.
As we demonstrate our discoveries we

Shall turn the jealousy of some to ire.
And then alternately be lionized
And dungeoned for our pains. Time's verdict will
Be made our epitaph. But what of that—
Whether the bubble Fame shall glitter in
Our eye and burst in death, or leave its mark
In marble on our grave? The age must move.

 L. Shall I assist you with your overcoat?
 N. First let us see the visage of the night.
Why, how dark! It rains a little, and it
Looks as though it might be raining ink and
Blotting out the earth. Here, I can spare my
Ulster, being provided for without it.
Thanks, I can get along without it.
 N.   But not
So well without as with. Put it on. There,
The storm will scarce discover where you are.
 L. That's lucky now. I'll go along with you.
 GILLESPIE. Seeing you have good company I guess
I'll take the street-car here, so say, good-night.
 N. Good-night. We'll talk away the distance and
Arouse to find our toes before the fire. (*They start.*)
 L. Very few people on the street.
 N.   No blame
For shirking close acquaintance with a night
Like this. 'Tis like a dun, whose face is not
So welcome as his back.
 L.   Persistent too,
Demanding vital energy, and will
Not be rebuffed.—How long do you suppose

Before our principles so far prevail
That they will shape society?
  N.   Truth, like
The dawn, moves not with measurable steps
That we can count by clock-ticks, but it steals
Across the tree-tops of men's minds and sinks,
Suffusively, until the vallies of
The soul become transfigured in its sheen.
Only as we compare the present with
The past can we perceive the progress made.
So will it be. But that our principles
Will yet prevail is certain as that day
Will follow night.
  L.   I'd like to linger o'er
This theme, as lovers on a moonlight night
Where they can hear their own hearts beat. But we
Lack moonlight; so I guess we'll have to part
As this is my way home.
  N.   That makes me think
Of what I overlooked on coming up
To meeting. I must call and see a man
Who lives on ninth. I'm sorry I forgot
It. But there is a compensation in
All ills; and this postpones our parting for
A block or two.
  L.   What a coincidence
Of blundering! or shall I simply say,
Forgetfulness? I have myself to keep
Right on and see a fellow I engaged
To meet at Strouth's hotel. And I shall have

To hurry too; so here we have to part. (*Exit
  Norton.*)
 L. Confound it! What a balk after so good
A start. But luck, like women, must be wooed.
Well, I shall have to find the boys and let
Them scatter to their homes. It hardly pays
To fish a night like this without a bite.
But what a pity, when the night seemed made
For such a job! This lets him off for once.
The second time may fail; but third makes up
For all. Luck seems to like the number three.—
The greasy hypocrite! He's but a wick.
And all we touch is just the tallow that
Has stuck to him in dipping. Oh!
But how his precious tongue has been perfumed!
H—hem! how nicely truth, philanthropy,
And all the other pretty words that take
With men as fashion-plates with women, drop
From his sweet lips as from a honeycomb!
But I must put some muscle in my step.
Let's see—they must be somewhere near. (*Snag
  and Black Joe come up behind. Big Bill
  at their heels. Lurk turns.*)
    Hello! (*He falls.*)
 B. B. By golly boys! its Lurk as sure as you're
Alive. It sounded like him when he holloed.
 B. S. Lurk or no Lurk, it's too dark to look for
Fleas. Leg it out of this. (*Snag and Black Joe
  run.*)
 B. B. I'll satisfy myself. (*He stoops and feels*

at the face.)

Thunder and lightning! it *is* him I swan.

Lew—Lew. Speak. Lew if it's you. (*Policeman approaches. Bill runs. Is pursued and caught.*)

Say boss, Where are you taking me?

POLICEMAN. Don't be too nice About your lodgings when you get them free. What have you done?

B. B. I don't know what we've done.

P. We! More than one was there?

B. B. Yes, Bob and Joe.

P. Bob and Joe who?

B. B. Golly! I don't know as I ought to tell. It wasn't me as did The job.

P. Of course not. No one ever has When caught. (*They pass the corpse.*)

A VOICE. Yes, dead enough; his head smashed in Behind.

P. So that's what *we* have done. Come on Before that crowd gets trooping after us. -(*Exeunt.*)

CHAPTER IV.

Scene—*On a levee and at a police Station.*
Slim Sam. What's up boys?
Jim Blake. They've nabbed Bob Snag and Black
   Joe for murder.
S. S. Murder! When?
J. B. Soon as they came
To work.
   S. S. By thunder! I must go and see
About it.
   J. B. See about it? What can you
See, eh?
   S. S. Get my place filled; that's all. (*Exit.*) It's no
Use, I must sit down here. The curse of hell
Be on the day that I had anything to do
With it! It is, and on all days, and on
Me too—the tarnel fool I was. I might
Have known that blood will stick and curse and
   curse
And stick as brimstone burns and blisters. It
Is burning in my bones. I feel it in
My very marrow, drying it. My back
Is weak; my legs are failing me; my flesh
Is shrinking. Just look there. (*Pinching his hand.*)

                        There's just enough—
And only just—to hold my bones together.—
Nabbed—both of them; and me as good as nabbed.
And then to think it didn't do a wink
To help us out, but seemed to help us in.
The Devil must have got me into this;
For I had natural sense enough to know
That Devil's work brings Devil's pay. But done
It is, and pay-day's here; and here I am,
A half-way murderer—the fool I was.
I wish that I could tear my carcass limb
From limb and throw it to the quarters of
The globe and put an end to such a fool.—
I wonder why that peeler looks so much
This way. He passes on. All right. And yet
I don't know; it will have to come. Two nabbed.
That means me too. The sooner I prepare
For it the better. As we're in for it
Things can't be worse; and life is sweet. I'll squeal
And save my neck, and that will lighten up
My lift without increasing theirs; for they
Are booked. It makes my heart beat lighter
As I think of it. Then that's the thing to do.
'Twill come the nearest to undoing what
Is done. But I will have to get the start
Of them or they may tell some yarn and get
Me fixed. They're not a bit too good for that.
    (*Goes to the police station.*)
I'm that other chap you want. (*To a policeman.*)
    POLICEMAN.   What other?

S. S.   That helped to kill Ben Boyle.
P.   Be careful what
You say. But come this way with me.
(*Before chief of Police.*)
CHIEF OF POLICE. What is your name?
S. S.   Sam Drew; but they call me,
Slim Sam.
CH' OF P. And you inform against yourself
That you were implicated in the crime
Of murder?
S. S.   I was there and gave a lift
To it, but didn't do the killing; and
If you'll let up a bit on one I'll tell
You everything you want to know.
CH' OF P.   What Boyle
Was this you killed? and when did it occur?
S. S. Ben Boyle. We killed him when the long-
     shore strike
Was on.
CH' OF P. That is enough. The officer
Will have you placed in custody until
The prosecutor shall arrive, take down
Your deposition, and investigate
The facts. Meanwhile, you are our prisoner.
SCENE—*In a cell.*
THEOPHRASTUS GRIPE, ATTORNEY AT LAW.
Well sir, without the best of help your chance
Of life is dear at one bad cent. I would
Not take your chances for a world—that is,
Without the very best of help. But I

Can see a way to bring you through and let
You snap a fillip in the face of Fate.
Now how much money can you raise?

    BOB SNAG.   I have
A lot and shanty that I bought when lots
Were cheap; and that is all I have.

    T. G.   That is
The lot your family is living on?

    B. S. Yes.

    T. G. Well, give me a deed of that and I
Will get you clear.

    B. S.   Then that will scoop me out.

    T. G. Sir, you are poised upon a needle's point,
And Death has got his finger on the strings
Of life to snap them with a jerk. This is
No time to halt and haggle o'er a bit
Of dirt, with which you buy your life. Decide—
Which is worth most to you, your lot or life?
Which would your wife prefer, a paltry bit
Of earth or him she called her sweetheart years
Ago? And which would pay your children best,
A father or a dirt-patch for a flock
Of geese? You know the worth of life to you
And them. So here is your alternative—
A deed, or dangle from a rope and leave
Your family a murderer's legacy.

    B. S. But can you clear me sure and certain?

    T. G.   Yes,
As sure as if it were already done;
For juries, now-a-days, are riddles, and

A shake that has enough of dollars at
Its back would sift the devil through and all
His imps—that is, when rightly done.
    B. S.   Agreed.
    T. G.   You say you helped to get away with
        Lurk—
But by mistake?
    B. S.   Yes, Norton had the spot.
    T. G.   You say that Lurk and you were friends?
    B. S.   Yes, chums.
And he's the very one that planned the thing;
And how he came to trap himself is more
Than I can tell.
    T. G.   And your accomplices
Were Black Joe and Big Bill. Were these the
        friends
Of Lurk?
    B. S.   As good as brothers any day.
    T. G.   Now are you certain no one saw you when
You did the deed?
    B. S.   As certain as I breathe.
The night was wet, and dark enough to snuff
Out fifty moons; and there was no one near—
At least, when I and Black Joe left; and trust
Big Bill for dawdling with the Devil at
His heels.
    T. G.   How came they to suspicion you?
    B. S.   They must have seen us going to the hall
Together.
    T. G.   If no more, you only have

To keep your mouth well corked and all will go
As smoothly as if we were Providence.

    T. G.   Did Big Bill go away with you?

    B. S.   No, he
Stepped back, suspecting it was Lurk was struck.
But Bill can care for number one.

    T. G.   If he
Was seen and recognized the clue is there,
In which case we must make another plea.
You say Lurk halloed?

    B. S.   He began to as
We struck him. One blow silenced him as quick
As if we'd chopped the sound square off; and down
He fell, kerwollop, like a log of wood.

    T. G.   Is Big Bill still at large?

    B. S.   I guess he is.
Soon as he heard that we were nabbed he'd go
By shank's express on everlasting time.

    T. G.   If he was recognized we'll have to watch
Our cards and keep them covered up. Our plea
Must be that you were going home, when Big
Bill, in the rear, heard Lurk and started back,
But, seeing others coming, ran away,
To keep himself untainted by suspicion.
I'll fix the story straight as tightened string,
And all of you must stick to it
As to a bob-tail chance of life.

    B. S.   No fear.

    T. G.   Well now, your deed. You have a copy, I
Suppose, at home?

B. S.   Yes, go and see my wife
And she will find it for you.
     T. G.   That's all right.
Now keep your hopes upon the topmost shelf,
And you'll be there as soon as Time can wink.

           SCENE—*In Bob Snag's Shanty.*

     MRS. SNAG. What must we do when we have lost
         our home ?
     THEOPHRASTUS GRIPE. What must you do when
         you're a widow and
Your children fatherless ?
     MRS. S.   Heaven only knows.
     T. G. It need not be. Your husband's life is at
Your own command, to forfeit or to save.
It cannot be you think so many feet
Of dirt too great a sacrifice to save
That husband's life. Just think of all the years
You yet may spend in wedded pleasure for
A paltry lot. Think how your children, in
A heartless world like this, have need of such
A father's care, and say if you would lose
For them the precious boon, when you can hold it
At so cheap a rate. The fact is, such
A lot as yours is scarcely worth the cost
Of making out a deed. But I would have
You feel the honest consciousness—the pride
Of having paid me something for my pains,
Which are the fruitage of my sympathy.
I do assure you madam, that my heart
Is aching for you in this trying hour.

To prove myself a friend when friendship is
Most worth, well knowing that you need a man
To help you keep the hunger-wolf away.
Hence, why I give you such an easy chance
To save a husband's and a father's life.

    Mrs. S. Yes, sir. I feel that all our lives are wrapt
In his. His grave would swallow all our hopes.
But then, you know, I couldn't help but think
A mother's thoughts and have a mother's fears.
And so it came to me this way: suppose
I thought, we lose our home, we lose our all;
And when all's gone, it's all, sir, sure enough;
And whether it was much or little aint
Worth breath enough to tell. It's plain, you know,
That nothing's nothing anyway.

    T. G.   I would
Not turn you out of house and home for lots
Like yours enough to make a continent;
Of that you may be sure.

    Mrs. S.   Forgive me, sir,
My question and accept my thanks for all
Your sympathy. I'm sure you're very kind.

    T. G. I always pride myself on being fair
And square—as fair as fair can be and square
Enough to keep affairs in shape. Well now,
The deed.

    Mrs. S. Yes sir; (*Searching in a trunk.*) It's here...

    T. G.   Now come with me;

Then we will get the matter all arranged,
And soon your husband shall be home again,
And all be lovely as the summer days. (*Exeunt.*)

   Scene.—*Big Bill in his cell.*

Warden. Some fellows are arrested, and they say
That you had part with them in killing one,
Ben Boyle, about a month ago.

 Big Bill.   What! have
They squealed?

 W. Of course. That's how we come to know.

 B. B. The tarnel cusses that they are! By Jo!
But won't I let 'em see that two can play
That game! It's Snag and Black Joe murdered Lurk
And got me hitched with them: only they missed
Their neighbor's dog and killed their own. And now
To think they squeal and lie on me!

 W.   See here;
That game's played out. Should half the stories told
Be true, this place would be a dove-cote and
The birds we get all white as angels' wings.
It might be fitly called, The saint's abode.

 B. B. But what I say is true—as true as I'm
A fool; and I am fool enough to make
A dozen fools out of or I'd never
Have been in with them. Dog on it; but I
Do believe that Norton's just a bully
Boy. Why, he gave us strikers all an X
A piece; which aint what every one would do.

But Lurk, he got his back up like a cat.
When dogs are round, and nothing else would do
But Norton must be killed; and some way, Lurk,
He happened when we looked for Norton, and
He got the whack that laid him out. That's so,
As sure as I'm in limbo. And you know,
There ain't a chance of doubting that.
    W.   Not much.
    B. B.   I guess they didn't tell that they them-
       selves
Killed Boyle. Slim Sam and me, we took a hand
In cornering him; but they topped off the job.
That's so. And now they come and squeal on me
And Sam to save their necks. There's Sam, he's had
His belly full of thunder ever since;
And so they wouldn't trust him on this job.
And if I'd had Sam's sense I'd not been here.
This is the pay I get for playing fool.
Well, somehow, fools get paid when pay-day comes.
       Scene—*Slim Sam in his cell.*
    Slim Sam. I swan, but you're the fellow was at
      the
Detective's lodgings when they found him dead.
    Trip. I guess I am. I learn you had a hand
In killing Boyle.
    S. S.   No, not in killing him;
But I was there.
    T.   Did the detective, as
You called that hunchback, have a hand in that
Affair?

S. S. The leading hand. He acted as
Decoy and got Boyle where we wanted him.
 T. Do you know Joblinsky?
 S. S. By sight; that's all.
 T. Had he a hand in it?
 S. S. He may have known
Of it through the detective. If he did,
That's all. What makes you ask me? Have they nabbed
Him too?
 T. No, not for that. But this time he
Turns out to be a *she*.
 S. S. You don't say that
Joblinsky is a woman?
 T. That's just it.
Russia has a long account to settle
With her if it could; but she is booked for
Devilment enough to settle her right
Here. Uncle Sam will foot her future bills.
 S. S. Well, that beats me that he should be a woman.

 · SCENE—*Bob Snag in his cell.*

THEOPHRASTUS GRIPE. It's my ill luck to bring unlucky news;
Not such as tolls the death-knell of your case,
Yet such as bids our wits be wide awake.
Big Bill's arrested, and he has uncorked
Himself.
 BOB SNAG. What, squealed?
 T. G. Yes, spilled out everything.

B. S.   That sends us all to Jericho.

T. G.   No, not
At all.   What kind of fellow is Big Bill?

B. S.   A great, green, lubbering gawky; tough as
A mule, with no more sense.

T. G.   The greener now
And less of sense the better for our case.

B. S.   Well, he's as green as Biddy's bonnet that
The old cow ate for cabbage.

T. G.   Lucky that.
What queer things have you noticed in him that
Would indicate a feeble mind?

B. S.   There's scarce
Enough of feeble mind, or any other mind,
To find with spectacles; but, gawky-like,
When others entertain his ear with talk,
He has an open, hungry-looking mouth,
And when their story, like the pointer of
A clock, has measured off its round, he gulps
It always with a smack and says, "That's so."

T. G.   Always.

B. S.   Yes; if he hadn't got Big Bill
For nickname we had christened him,   That's so.

T. G.   I've got my cue.   This answer has become
A habit; and the habit, working on
So weak a mind, becomes a source of strange
Hallucinations, so that when his nerves
Become perturbed by some unusual shock,
As 'twas in case of his arrest, it is
By instinct he responds to any charge,

"That's so." Moreover, what he knows of men
And things is so associated with this
Habit of assent that he is but
The parrot of an automatic mind.
That argument, elaborated with
Rhetoric art, will scoop a jury-box
And put the jurors in your stocking, like
So many candy-sticks at christmas-tide,
Making me *Santa-claus*. So, after all,
You see, we've got our grip upon the horns
Of Luck. Now, inventory, ere I come
Again, the things you know him to have said
Or done that have a smack of crankiness,
And I will turn the crank to good account.
    B. S. I guess you know the kinks.
    T. G.   Trust me for that.
That's 'cuteness sir; and 'cuteness prods the ribs
Of law and picks her pocket while she laughs.
Our province is to tangle witnesses
Until, when all is o'er, they are themselves
Amazed to con the evidence they gave,
And to make jurors give their ears the lie
And suck our sophistries like sugar plums—
The thing you need in such a scrape as this.
Well now, good day. I shall be back within
A week at most, and, in the meantime, try
To see Big Bill and make the most of him. (*Exit.*)
    WARDEN. What sort of client have you got in there?
We've got a fellow here who charges him
With killing some one else—one Boyle.

T. G. What! Where?

W. Boyle, a longshoreman, when the strike was
on.

T. G. Is that a fact?

W. It's fact that he has made
An affidavit to it as a fact.

T. G. How does he know?

W. He says that he was there,
Particeps criminis, but charges Snag
And one Joe Black as principals.

T. G. Then I
Must make inquiries into this. (*Returns to the cell.*)
I guess
You'll think me body-servant to ill-luck.
But here a warden tells me that they have
A fellow charging you with killing one
Named Boyle. What is there to it? Anything?

B. S. By thunder! too much for a fellow's good.
Who is it that they've got?

T. G. He says that he
Took part in it.

B. S. Slim Sam, I'll bet, for he's
Been belly-aching over it a month
And more, and wanted thirty hours a day
To gripe it out. He's just a granny noodle.
Well, that does the job sure. I may as well
Give up.

T. G. Tut tut! Never give up until
They swing you up. But don't be scared. Your life
Is worth a good insurance yet. Tell me

The worst that I may know what I will have
To meet.

    B. S.   Well, it was in the strike. Big Bill,
Slim Sam, Black Joe and me, we did the job
For him; and he deserved it too—the scab
He was.

    T. G.   And did *you* do the killing?

    B. S.   Yes—
Me and Black Joe.

    T. G.   That complicates affairs.
But let me see. There must be some way out.
       (*Walks the floor.*)
Was either of your parents any time
Insane, or given to freaks of oddity,
That you can prove?

    B. S.   No, not that I'm aware.

    T. G.   Nor yet a grandparent on either side?

    B. S.   I never heard.

    T. G.   Nor uncle, aunt or cousin?

    B. S.   My mother had a cousin wasn't as
She ought to be.

    T. G.   Ah! *she*—a mental weakness on
The female side. Heredity will let
Its secrets out by an unerring law;
And all the worse when the parental life
Is operating, through gestative mouths,
In giving bias to its fetal ward.
Now stretch your memory to the twanging point,
And tell me what you have been told of her
Receiving some unusual scare or shock,

While yet your life was hers and sensitive
To all the fluctuations of her moods.

 B. S.   I well remember having heard her say,
That four months ere my birth, a wolfish dog
Attacked her, when a passer-by drove off
The brute and left her trembling almost at
The fainting point, from which effect she scarce
Recovered for a week.

 T. G.   That hook will do
To hang a jury on.   You see, the shock to her
Mentality at that precarious stage
In your development, ere yet your traits
Of mind unalterably were posited,
Disturbed your mental equipoise and gave,
Through an unfortunate heredity,
A timid fear that has developed to
A constitutional aggressiveness
Against imaginary foes, and which,
In its exaggerated caprices,
Spares not your dearest friends, as, instance, Lurk.

 B. S.   What! would you make me out a lunatic?

 T. G.   An expedient stroke of policy, enough
To fool a jury with.   You can afford
To be a little crazy for your life.
Moreover, wé can have revenge on him
Who turned informer, and suggest that he
Employed you as his tool to do the job
For him and save his neck from feeling hemp.

 B. S.   I guess they'd have to cull a county for
A dozen fools who could be fooled that way.

T. G. Of course, 'tis fools we get in such a place,
The mental hulks 'gainst whose dull brains the tides
Of knowledge wash and leave them anchored still
In ignorance. To get such is a fine
Art practiced in extremity. Pleas of
Insanity awake their sympathy
And agitate them like so many ewes
That hear their lambs bleat in the butcher's pen.
The greater fool the better juryman.
    B. S. That seems to give me but a flimsy chance.
    T. G. Flimsy or not it is a chance; and in
A case like this—with talent at one end
And but an average jury at the other—
One thread of gossamer mere strong enough
To pull you through a cambric-needle's eye.
Then keep good heart. When anyone comes here,
Look wild. Stare like a dead fish. Threaten him;
But don't say anything too sensible. (*Exit.*)
    B. S. I'm in for it at last. It's no use. No
One's dunderhead enough to swallow what
He says. I don't myself half understand
The mixed-up stuff. Then how can such a set
Of fools as those he talks about? Or if
They be not fools, what use is all this bosh?
There's too much fact for anything so thin
To hide. I may as well play smash and blab
It all, then trust to luck to save my neck.
I've heard of men escaping who confess;
Then in a a while a mandlin Governor comes
And pardons in a tender mood. Who knows

But there may be the shadow of a chance?
      Scene—*In Gripe and Sharp's office.*
   Theophrastus Gripe. In Snag's case we must
      have the jury hung
Or he will hang. I wish you'd make it in
Your way to see the sheriff and suggest
Some names. There's Blunderbuss, who, like a hog,
Will go according as they pull his tail;
And Flip, who knows whatever others don't
And proves them fools by doing as they don't;
And Sloan, who needs a month to hem and haw
And then conclude he can't make up his mind;
And Kant, who has so soft a heart he would
Not hurt the snake that killed his *neighbor's* child;
And Prue, who sees a thousand ghosts of doubt
And dare not act until the last is laid;
And Veer, who tries to trim his sails to all
And yields to him who has the gustiest lungs;
And Schleiman, of the corner store, who found
In Snag, no doubt, a steady customer;
And Plod, whose fellow-feeling calculates
That mercy comes from being merciful;
And Reasor, who believes a man insane
Whene'er he takes away his fellow's life;
And Tellman—
   Newsboy.   Morning Times.
   T. G.   (*Reading.*)   By jupiter!
What's this? Bob Snag confessed. (*Reads aloud.*)
                     Last night Bob Snag
Confessed to having helped to murder Lurk

And Boyle. We hope to have the details for
Our evening issue." So ends the case of Snag.
And what an everlasting fool! Well, let
Him swing; 'twill help to keep the ropemaker
In work. Born fools will die as they were born.

SCENE—*Mrs. Snag's door.*

SIMON GRUB. I give you notice to vacate the place
Within a month.

MRS. SNAG. What do you mean?

S. G. I mean
That you must leave before a month is gone,
Or I shall have to help you out of here.

MRS. S. Now who are you to come and mock a worse
Than widowed woman? Just as though I'd not
Enough to bear; and sure you don't so much
As own a grain of sand about the place.

S. G. Not quite so crank. Though not the
  owner quite,
I am the owner's fist; and that you'll feel
When it has struck your jib, as strike it will
If you are here when I come round again.

MRS. S. I don't believe a syllable of what
You say, you tantalizing knave. Go home
And pick the bedbugs off yourself, instead
Of worrying one who has enough to bear.

S. G. I guess your eyes will open when I come
Again.

MRS. S. A gentleman intends to get
My husband off; and so we let him have
The place; and he has promised me to let

Me stay. He was so kind, and talked with such
A heart, I know he wouldn't turn us out
Of here. He said he wouldn't for a world
Of lots like this; and he's a gentleman.

    S. G. Well no, I guess he wont; for he has sold
It out to Ghoul and Company, and I
Am agent for the firm; and in their name
I give you notice that you have to leave.
Here is the notice written in due form
Of law.

    Mrs. S. My God! you don't say that.

    S. G.   That's just
Exactly what I say. And what is more,
I mean it with a vim. Read what you've got
And say if that don't look like business now.

    Mrs. S. Oh my! what shall we do? You
        wouldn't turn
A woman out of house and home, with four
Small children clinging to her skirts, would you?

    S. G. Our firm is not responsible for sex;
And as to brats, the market's beared with them.
And business bored; from which you may infer
We've no quotations on the article.

    Mrs. S. But is not pity still in human breasts?
Has poverty no speech that human ears
Can hear; misfortune no strong heart-key to
Unlock your sympathy; and tears no power
To melt the icebergs of your arctic soul?
Even a dog could understand our woes;
And, understanding, it would pity us.

S. G.   In that we do not have dog's ways. We do
Not deal in slobber but estate.   Our firm
Has paid a round five-hundred for this lot
And wants to build on it; so you must move.
   Mrs. S.   Five hundred! and he said it wasn't worth
The cost of making out a deed.
   S. G.   Indeed!
   Mrs. S.   But this is all of earth that we have had.
Where are we to move to?
   S. G.   My gracious! do
You think 'twas me that married you?   Am I
Your husband? Did you ever find me in
Your bed? And must that squad of sticky brats
Come trooping at my heels and call me *Pap*,
That you would have me tell you where to go?
Go where you will; but go, as I have said.
   Mrs. S.   You are a hard, unfeeling man.
   S. G.   Add *cash*
And then you've got me figured out—*hard cash*,
With just so much of feeling as can feel
That it is hard; but none to run to waste.
In that, you see, we use economy.
We wouldn't have enough to cover all;
And so we use our feelings sparingly.
   Mrs. S.   God pity us when men are worse than brutes!
   S. G.   Well, see you're missing when the month is up.   (*Exit.*)

SCENE—*In Snag's cell.*

NORTON. And so 'twas me you meant to kill instead
Of Lurk.

BOB SNAG. To tell the honest truth, it was.

N. The honest truth is all the truth there is;
For truth is always honest. Tell me now,
In what had I offended you that you
Should seek so fearful a revenge?

B. S. Nothing.
I was a fool that let another lead
Me round to do what I had never thought
Of for myself. 'Twas Lurk that put us up
To it; and now he has his pay, and ours
Will come.

N. And what could Lurk have that should make
His bosom a volcano, hot with hate
And ready thus to belch forth fatal fire?

B. S. Why, nothing in the world but jealousy;
And that, somehow, is like a devil in
A man, that never lets him rest, but keeps
A-raking up hell-fire in him; hence he,
While meaning evil, credits others with
The same; since what he knows himself to be
He thinks they are. You know his restless eye.
Which, like a compass-needle, danced within
Its socket. Wickedly it twinkled as
He talked to us of blood—so cool—without
A muscle twitching in his face to hint
A possible compunction. I have been,

Myself a tough case, I confess; but I
Could never hide the fact that what I did
Was ripping like a dull saw at my heart.
But somehow, Lurk—he seemed to have a spell
Of deviltry that charmed and chained us to
His will. I guess it's bloody luck to have
One's wickedness come back upon him with
A spring and slap him in the face.
  N.   It is
A universal law that sin, like an
Infuriate rattlesnake, should bite itself
And die. But I am sorry you were led
Astray and brought to this.
  B. S.   And so am I.
But this is tardy penitence for one
Whose hands are doubly dyed with blood. Thus much
However, I may say; I have no more
Against you than an unborn babe can have
Against its mother. You have been a friend
To all of us; and I would thank you for
It if it didn't seem to savor of
Hypocrisy. But that is how I feel.
As for myself, I guess I'll have to pay
For blood with blood. All else is gone—all—all.
I'm but a cipher on the slate of life,
Waiting the hangman's sponge to wipe me out.
Even my wife and children are not mine,
Except as is the memory of a dream—
Enough to make me think of them and groan.
I had a home; but that is gone to pay

A lawyer, who can do me now no good;
And he has sold it. They have notice to
Vacate the premises within a month.
I felt that Fortune knocked me down before.
In that, she grinds me with her heel and seems
To threaten vengeance after death. Well, it's
Deserved. That thought lends poison to the sting
Of death. Were they provided for it would
Relieve my pillow of a thousand thorns.

    N. He did a heartless thing.
    B. S.   My only right
Is misery; and the tithe I get will but
Be interest on the misery that my deeds
Have caused to others. So let troubles come.
They will but be as mountains heaped upon
A grave that holds a coffined life. But I
Do wish the living might not have so large
A share of suffering through my fault.
    N.   Well now,
Be easy on that score. Your family
Shall be provided with a home. I'll see
To that myself.
    B. S. Why now, you don't mean that.
    N. Exactly that, to the last letter of
The final word.
    B. S.   It isn't nature to
Bestow a blessing when a curse is so
Well earned.
    N. 'Tis the sublimest triumph of
Our wisdom when we light our actions at

The throne of God and let them burn with pure
Divinity. Were He whose eye can pierce
The soul's sea-depths inexorable in
The meting us according to our ill
Desert, mankind were sore distraught. It is
In mercy that the world finds hopes; since that
Wards off the sword of justice from our souls.
Now, as I hope to share the greater boon
I give the less.
    B. S.   Why, you're a riddle, and
The more I see the less I understand
The mystery of the goodness in your heart,
Which, by its contrast, makes my badness look
The worse. Oh that I could but tell the boys
How good you are! For if they only knew,
They all would rally round you to a man.
    N. I shall be what I am whatever they
May be. But should they fail to understand
Me now; the echo of my message will
Be heard above my grave, and heeded then.
    B. S. I hope it may before. Well, you are breath
To me; for I can breathe more freely than
Before. This world is but a shriveled pod,
From which I soon shall drop—an unripe seed.
Life's wintry blasts forestall my autumn tide.
    N. Then seize the world before, and so escape
A second loss, which, since eternal, were
The greater by infinity.
    B. S.   I would
If one might dare to hope who needs to fear.

N. It is not daring when the heart is right.
B. S. But mine is black as night with murderers blood,
Which calls for vengeance with an awful voice.
N. Yet not so loud but Mercy's ear can hear
The voice of penitence though whispered low.

SCENE—*In court*.

THE JUDGE. Prisoners at the bar. It is my painful
Duty to announce, that in your case the
Jury has returned a verdict—guilty;
Which was the only verdict possible.
Your guilt is clear and albeit self-confessed.
Your double crime is most revolting to
Our sensibilities—the highest in
The category recognized by law;
Which justly makes your crime the pattern for
Your penalty, by taking from you the
Equivalent of what you took, so far
As guilt, in suffering, offsets innocence.
You well deserve more than a double death
For double murder. Less than what your hands
Have meted were a stint of justice, save
As you have one life, and one alone, to
Give. Were my feelings such as your offence
Would gender, I might now exult to speak
For justice and command your taking off;
Since you have outraged every attribute
Of true humanity. Two souls, whose hands
Were busy with life's vulgar drudgeries,
Without a moment to prepare for that

Momentous change which comes at best with dread
And solemn visage to us all, were rushed
To their account. Prepared or unprepared
You neither asked nor cared. And that which gives
Your guilt its blackest hue is this: Your crimes
Were not committed when the tempests of
The soul were rolling passion's thunders o'er
The conscience; when the judgment shook with shocks
Of sudden phrenzy, and the will was in
A tremor of suspense and hesitance,
Yet driven by blind impetuosity.
No, you deliberated on your deeds;
You looked at them; you measured, planned and then
You executed, with relentlessness
So cool it proves that pity has no home
With you; which leaves but little room for an
Appeal to pity in your case. No odds
That in the case of Lurk your blow glanced from
Another head to his. We ask the deed and not
The victim of the deed. You murdered, as
You meant; but Norton in the *form*
Of Lurk. Still, I remember that there is
This double stain upon your souls, and that
You are but ill-prepared to meet the Judge
Who sees your crime with keener eye than mine.
Your own, however, is the guilt who did
The deeds, and yours must be the consequence.
I must maintain the majesty of law

And vindicate the rights of innocence.
And now one only task remains to me,
Which is, to pass upon you severally
The sentence of the law. You Robert Snag
And Joseph Black, must hang, each by his neck,
Till dead; and may the Lord have mercy on
Your souls. In view of circumstances that
Appear to mitigate their guilt, the court
Will lay a lighter hand on Samuel Drew
And William Jinks. Its sentence is, that they
Shall be imprisoned for their natural life;
And may their hearts incline to better ways.

A PSALM OF FAITH.

PART I.

No threnodies have I to sing
   And, by their implication,
Against the Sovereign Ruler bring
   A covert accusation.

While He has daily led me on
   His blessings have been plenty;
Yet oft, alas, I saw not one
   While yet receiving twenty.

And though the stars were overhead,
   And the round moon had risen,
My timorous tears I freely shed
   Till they obscured my vision.

And oft, when pride has longed to scale
   Some lofty elevation,
He kept me groping in the vale
   Of deep humiliation.

My lot had thus been otherwise,
   Had I been first consulted;
But what has been I learn to prize
   From that which has resulted.

That otherwise had been as wise
    Is very far from certain.
Enough that His omnicient eyes,
    Which look behind the curtain.

Behold the meshes of the past
    And present as related
To that great future which shall last,
    And to all things created.

In safety I may say thus much:
    The network of creation
Is one great whole, whose parts, as such,
    Can have no isolation.

And time is one, whose years as beads
    Upon one string are threaded;
And each toward some conclusion leads
    That need not now be dreaded.

Had I first recognized His hand,
    His unseen wisdom trusted,
Affairs had then, at His command,
    Been differently adjusted.

For He fails not the best to give
    In all our circumetances;
But best at best is relative,
    As measured by the chances.

Before I braved the mountain road
    I needed strength and training;
Yet blindest ignorance I shewed,
    By constantly complaining.

At length, while yet I saw it not,
   My pathway was ascending;
And e'en the zig-zags in my lot
   Were toward the summit tending.

Thus while, with introspective eye,
   To self I thought to pander,
He led me towards a destiny
   Where life is broader, grander.

As I have will to follow up,
   And as I understand best,
I still approach the mountain top,
   Where life is broadest, grandest.

And what for me He seeks to do,
   And what has consummated,
He has as certainly in view
   For man as aggregated.

The lesson He is teaching me
   To other minds He teaches;
The goodness that I daily see
   To worthier millions reaches.

Those millions He is leading now,
   As me He has been leading.
Some brave ones near the mountain's brow,
   And others are proceeding.

A lifetime it requires for me
   To learn what He is teaching;
So must the world *its* lifetime be,
   Toward its great ideal reaching.

But fear again our faith debars
    From all that can avail us;
And so again we miss the stars
    And make the full-moon fail us.

For down we look to what is low,
    And see the lowest only,
And still more pessimistic grow,
    Since goodness looks so lonely.

But Providence is not asleep,
    Though man may be dyspeptic.
And let us wail or let us weep
    His ways are antiseptic.

Admit that earth has too few smiles,
    Too much of sin and sorrow,—
We must be many moral miles
    From Sodom and Gomorrah.

And all the intervening space
    Has had a slight ascension;
Though clock-like may have been our pace,
    And dull our apprehension.

Or else, the change that skill has wrought
    No real good possesses;
Or else, experience goes for nought,
    Nor art nor knowledge blesses.

But own we must a growth of mind,
    Improvement in condition;
Some evils have been left behind,
    And some are in transition.

And, clock like, we are moving still,
    With sure and forward motion,
Impelled by the Eternal Will,
    Whate'er our human notion.

Admit a void, in which the mind
    Is tentatively groping—
A chaos, where are millions, blind,
    Half doubting and half hoping.

A Power is brooding over all;
    And there is indication
That what we blindly chaos call
    Is incomplete creation.

The denser vapors are dispersed,
    Till light with mist is blended;
And yet will come the glory-burst
    Of orbs whose sheen is splendid.

There must be truth and certainty,
    As there are doubt and error.
There must be love and harmony,
    As there are strife and terror.

Nay, all the good we have in life
    Demonstrates their existence;
And in the very fact of strife
    Is proof of their persistence.

And partial good already gained
    By them in their vocation,
Is earnest of the whole obtained
    When comes the consummation.

PART II.

Whose eye can sweep the breadths of space
    And see—what most deem cryptic—
Where moves the moral world, can trace
    God's plans in their ecliptic.
Those plans are moving towards a goal,
    Without a shade of swerving;
And human nature as a whole
    Is some great purpose serving.

It is a solar orb within
    The universe of being;
Though, at its best, the spots of sin
    We cannot fail of seeing.

The goal defies our telescope,
    The spots our explanation;
And yet His nature gives us hope,
    His wisdom expectation.

And here, that hope to ratify,
    That expectation strengthen,
The beams that on our pathway lie
    Still broaden as they lengthen.

And since six thousand years of time
    Begin to elevate us,
They are a pledge of things sublime
    That certainly await us.

Six thousand multiplied by six,
  In ages of progression,
Must bring some grand climacterics,
  And give a great possession.

Already we the pressure feel
  Of greater power impelling,—
A quickening impetus to zeal,
  The world's great bosom swelling.

And when the pillories of the past—
  The heirlooms of oppression,
In which we hold our brothers fast,
  Impeding their progression ;—

When these shall all be laid aside,
  And we who now oppress them
Put off the kid gloves of our pride,
  To stimulate and bless them ;

When we are ready to obey
  Great Nature's *magna charter*,
Nor longer make the weak our prey,
  As chattles fit for barter ;—

The universal Father then
  Will bless us in our blessing ;
And all will prosper more than when
  One-half was half oppressing.

A mystery it has been that we
  Have found it hard to ravel ;
Why every birth of good should be
  With keenest pangs of travail.

Perchance the cost may make the boon
    Appear a greater treasure,
And the result more opportune,
    With its excess of pleasure.

But 'since 'tis thus that Nature gains
    Her greatest acquisitions,
We need not shudder at the pains
    Preceding new conditions.

It must be the Supreme presides
    Above the moral forces.
And guides them as the stars He guides
    Upon their silent courses.

And there is pent in moral force
    Repulsion and attraction,
To help obedience on its course,
    And smite sin with reaction.

Those forces we perceive in play,
    As with a tidal motion,
In rolling on some little bay;
    He views and moves the ocean.

Here, in the general tide of things,
    The flood is onward flowing;
Nor see we all the ships it brings,
    Nor know how far 'tis going.

But as we see the broken waves
    Recede along the beaches,
Still others come, as from their graves,
    With mightier upreaches.

And every crispy rolling crest
    That into gem-dust crumbles,
Is pledge and proof of all the rest,
    As on the sands it tumbles.

Nor is it much for Him to wait,
    Whose eye sees all the ages,
Whose finger wrote the book of fate,
    With centuries for its pages.

Enough for us that He is good,
    So far as comprehended;
And were the rest but understood,
    Our doubts were, doubtless, ended.

www.ingramcontent.com/pod-product-compliance
Lightning Source LLC
Chambersburg PA
CBHW030248170426
43202CB00009B/664